STONESETTING

for Contemporary Jewelry Makers

ST. MARTIN'S GRIFFIN
NEW YORK

STONESETTING FOR CONTEMPORARY JEWELRY MAKERS. Text copyright © 2012 by Melissa Hunt. All rights reserved. Printed in China. For information, address St. Martin's Press, 175 Fifth Avenue, New York, N.Y. 10010.

www.stmartins.com

Library of Congress Cataloging-in-Publication Data Available Upon Request

ISBN: 978-1-250-01532-7

First U.S. Edition: December 2012

10 9 8 7 6 5 4 3 2 1

Commissioning Editor: Isheeta Mustafi

Art Director: Emily Portnoi

Art Editor: Jennifer Osborne

Design Concept: Emily Portnoi

Layout: Emma Atkinson

Cover Design: Emily Portnoi

Cover images: (front cover, left to right) Erin Staples, Elaine Cox, Anne Malone (back cover, left to right) Konstanze Kraus, Liaung Chung Yen, Erin Staples

Picture Research: Heidi Adnum

Illustrations: Anthony Atkinson, Peters & Zabransky, Emily Portnoi

Photography on pages 38–59: Michael Wicks

Tools and Metals supplied by Cookson Precious Metals

Gemstones supplied by A. E. Ward & Son

STONESETTING

for Contemporary Jewelry Makers

TECHNIQUES, INSPIRATION, AND PROFESSIONAL
ADVICE FOR STUNNING RESULTS

Melissa Hunt

TABLE OF CONTENTS

INTRODUCTION

The opportunity to write a book about stonesetting enabled me to refine the techniques I was already familiar with, but also reminded me of how much more there is to know about the relationship between gemstones and metals.

This book begins with a guide to the essential tools and equipment you'll need followed by a directory of the most commonly used gemstones. Both traditional and less-conventional stonesetting techniques are explained, along with valuable information about the compatibility of stones and metals. Each step-by-step tutorial has a recommendation about the skill level involved (beginner, intermediate, or advanced), and includes handy tips for varying the setting and producing great results.

I spent my childhood on the South Devon coast in England, collecting sea-worn fragments and watching the effects of erosion. After training at the London Metropolitan University, I valued the opportunity of using my knowledge of jewelry fabrication techniques to create wearable pieces from the objects I had gathered as a child. I hope this book will inspire you to adapt the techniques and create your own beautiful designs.

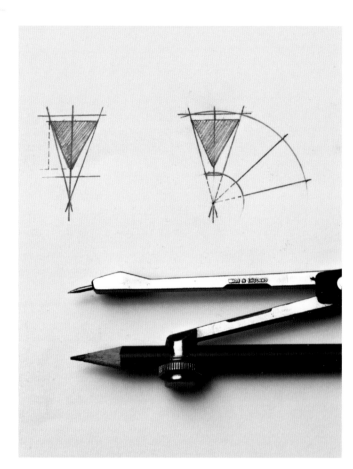

TOOLS & MATERIALS

CHAPTER 1
EQUIPMENT

OPPOSITE
PAGE
The author's bench
and studio.

Jewelry-making tools are objects for a maker to get to know and love—through time and wear, these tools develop unique curves, shapes, and cuts produced by the way that their owner uses and stores them. Buying cheap tools is a false economy—treat yourself to the most expensive tool kit you can afford and you will see the superior results produced.

THE BENCH AND STUDIO

THE JEWELER'S BENCH: This should be 37in (95cm) in height and screwed to the wall to reduce movement. Sit so that you are at shoulder height to the bench, at around eye level or just above the work. Invest in a leather benchskin to hang underneath the scooped-out area in the bench: this will hold tools and catch metal filings and dropped stones.

An angle-poise lamp with a daylight bulb is a necessity.

Consider where soldering will take place (torches are often held in the nondominant hand), the location of power and electrical equipment, and where tools will be stored.

A screwed-down vise with easy access from all angles is also very useful. Make a quick drawing of your studio layout to find the best place for the pickle (should be warm, ventilated, and close to a sink), rolling mill (will need clearance to wind), polishing motor (polishing dust must be contained and kept away from computers and liquids), pendant motor, bench drill, and a safe area for storing chemicals.

MEASURING AND MARKING TOOLS

SCRIBER: Steel-pointed tool that scribes marks onto metal. Store on its side to prevent blunting the tip.

CENTER PUNCH: Used with a cow hide mallet to produce an indentation in metal. Automatic center punches are used without a mallet.

DIVIDERS: For drawing arcs, dividing circles, and marking out lengths.

STEEL RULER: More resilient than a plastic ruler, these are invaluable for measuring and marking out.

RING GAUGE: Used for taking an accurate ring size. The correct gauge should "walk" over the second knuckle of the finger, and rotate when it reaches the base of the finger.

ENGINEER'S SQUARE: For checking right angles and straight edges. Place the corner or edge of a workpiece into the inside of the square and hold up to the light to check for gaps.

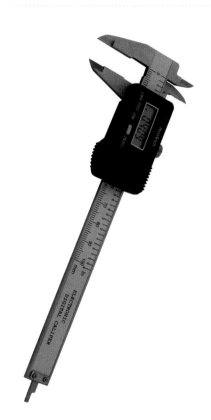

VERNIER GAUGE: Used for scoring parallel lines, measuring stones, thicknesses of metal, internal dimensions, and depths of tubing. Digital slide guides are more accurate than nondigital.

BANGLE SIZER: Measures the length of metal required to make a bangle.

DIGITAL SCALES: For weighing stones, weighing metal for hallmarking, and quoting for commissions.

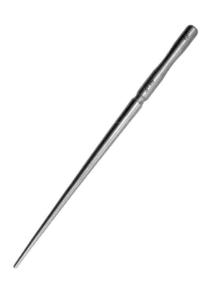

RING MANDREL: Tapered rod used for making rings to size. Available in wood, steel, or aluminum.

TRIBLETS: Available in round, oval, and other profiles, these tapered steel tools are used for making settings round.

ROUND MARKED GROOVED MANDREL: Useful for resizing and reshaping stone-set rings. Has a D-shaped groove running along its length to house the stone while working on the piece.

BANGLE MANDREL: Used for fabricating bangles. Available in wood or steel, round and oval.

DIXIEME GAUGE: For measuring wall thicknesses—especially useful for a surface of an irregular density. Also measures internal areas, but not with such accuracy.

PUNCHES, BLOCKS, AND ROLLING MILL

STEEL BLOCK: All-purpose flat, smooth block for checking straight edges, hammering textures, and cooling metal.

DRAWPLATE: Used for straightening, work hardening, and reducing the size and profile of wire and rod. Also used to make tubing. Needs to be secured in a vise.

LETTER AND NUMBER PUNCHES: Steel punches that make the impression of a letter, number, or shape in annealed metal. Use with a hide mallet with the workpiece on a steel block.

DAPPING PUNCHES AND BLOCK: Spherical punches of different sizes make an annealed disc domed by placing it in an appropriately-sized cutout in a dapping block and hammering with a hide mallet. Also useful for "trueing up" rings by placing in the dapping block and tapping with a dapping punch on the ring's horizontal plane.

SWAGE BLOCK: Used to produce tubing or half tubing from annealed sheet by using a former such as the handle of a dapping block on its side.

ROLLING MILL: Used for making sheet metal and wire thinner and for impressing textures.

DISC CUTTER: Punches that cut out circles or make circular marks on metal.

HAND TOOLS

ROUND-NOSE PLIERS: Used in chain making, these are great for producing coils of wire that can then be cut up into jump rings. Tapered, so can produce small wire rings of different sizes.

FLAT-NOSE PLIERS: Used to produce rectangular jump rings and for holding pieces.

D-SHAPE OR HALF-ROUND PLIERS: One side of the jaws is cresent-shaped toward the center and the other flat. When used with the curved side on the inside of a ring, they help encourage it into a round shape. Can also produce larger jump rings than round-nose pliers.

SNIPE-NOSE PLIERS: Used for creating small angles in wire, such as square jump rings, and for holding work flat.

PARALLEL-ACTION PLIERS: These strong-jawed pliers work in a way that their jaws open in a parallel spacing, as opposed to the v-shaped action of the pliers described above. This makes them very strong jawed.

CUTTING TOOLS

END OR TOP CUTTERS: Does a similar job to side cutters, but from a different angle.

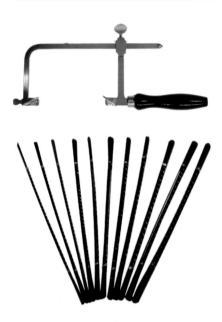

PIERCING SAW FRAME AND BLADES: Used for cutting sheet, rod, wire, and internal shape fretwork. Blade sizes vary from 4/0 (thickest gauge with teeth far apart) to 8/0 (thinnest gauge with teeth close together). A good medium size is 2/0.

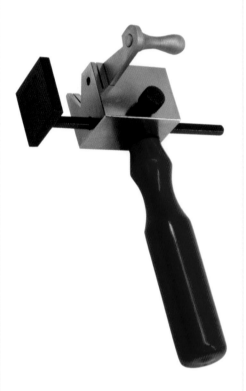

TUBE CUTTER, SPECIAL JOINT TOOL, OR CHENIER CUTTER: Holds rod and tubing so that they can be accurately cut to set lengths. Has a slot to ensure the piercing saw blade is kept true. Some models also cut angles.

TAP AND DIE SET: Used to create threads on male and female parts to enable one to screw in and out of the other.

LUBRICANTS: Drill bits, piercing saw blades, and stonesetting burrs can be kept sharp during use with machine oil, beeswax, or WD40 spray. Lubricants also prevent rust.

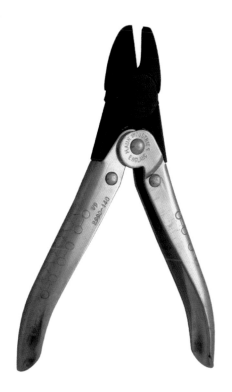

TIN SNIPS: Used for cutting solder and thin sheet, the blades close by crossing over one another. Avoid cutting binding wire with these, as it will skid down the blades and blunt them.

SIDE CUTTERS: The blades of these close by meeting, as opposed to crossing over each other, so they can make a flush cut in thin wire with a slight bevel.

HAMMERS AND MALLETS

RIVETING HAMMER: Can create tiny texture marks in annealed metal and splay the head of a rivet.

PLANISHING HAMMER: Has a shallow domed face and a flat face for texturing and planishing annealed metal.

CHASING HAMMER: Traditionally used to emboss metal from the front, sometimes with punches, this hammer has shallow domes on both faces.

JOBBING OR BALL-PEIN HAMMER: Has one domed face and one flat face. A good all-rounder, used to create textures in annealed metal.

RAISING HAMMER: Has two rectangular faces and is used to "raise" annealed silver over a stake or in a sand bag to create shapes and forms.

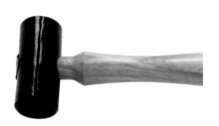

COWHIDE MALLET: A soft-headed but hard-wearing mallet made of spiralled and stapled lengths of cowhide. Different head weights are available.

REPOUSSÉ HAMMER: Traditionally used to emboss metal from the reverse, sometimes with punches, this hammer is also used for forming and planishing annealed metal against stakes or a sand bag. Also good for texturing annealed metal and splaying rivet heads.

TEXTURE HAMMERS: Ready-textured heads of a variety of patterns such as circles, squares, and straight lines, which impress these shapes into annealed metal.

WOODEN BOSSING MALLET: Used in the initial stages of raising a silversmithed piece in a sandbag, it has a small dome at one side and a wider dome at the other for shaping and trueing metal.

FILES

HAND FILES: Large files used for forming and smoothing metal. Available in various cuts and profiles including flat, half-round, round (tapered), and triangular. They are much easier to use with a wooden handle attached.

NEEDLE FILES: Packs of six small assorted files in a variety of cuts and profiles: round, half-round, three square, four square, flat, and warding. Good for refining edges, internal shapes, and difficult to reach places.

ESCAPEMENT FILES: Very fine cut needle files used for intricate and detailed work.

EMERY PAPER: Abrasive papers of different grades that, when used in succession (medium to fine) remove deep scratches and prepare the workpiece for polishing or applying a matte finish. Available in grades from 180 (coarse) to 2,500 (very fine, for polishing), commonly used grades are those between 600 and 2,000. They have a number on the reverse referring to the proximity of the abrasive particles; work through as many grades as possible for a superior finish. Used taped around an emery stick, wrapped around needle files, or slotted into a split pin in a pendant motor.

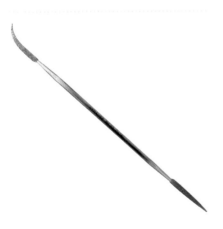

RIFFLER FILES: Small files with curved and furled ends to refine edges and remove specific areas of metal.

SOLDERING EQUIPMENT

BINDING WIRE: Used to hold seams and joining parts together during soldering. Most types of binding wire need to be removed before pickling.

TORCH: Sievert torches run on propane or butane gas, but are expensive and take up space. A good quality chef's blow torch is suitable for most annealing and soldering jobs; these run on lighter fuel.

BORAX CONE, CERAMIC DISH, AND BRUSH: Used to keep the immediate soldering area free of dirt and oxides. The cone grinds away with a little water in the dish to create a paste the consistency of light cream, which is painted onto the join in the workpiece with a sable brush.

SOLDERING BLOCKS: Available as asbestos substitute, charcoal, or perforated. Most can be broken up into smaller bits to prop up workpieces. The choice of material is down to personal preference: dressmaking pins can be temporarily inserted into asbestos substitute to hold work in place before soldering, charcoal is good for better visibility of solder and creating craters to specific shapes with a stonesetting burr in a pendant motor, and perforated blocks let more heat travel around the piece. Retain the shape of a charcoal block by wrapping it with binding wire before soldering.

AUFLUX/AUROFLUX: Liquid flux used predominantly with gold, but can also be used with other metals. Can be mixed with borax.

SOLDER: Usually bought in a strip, grades of hard, medium, and easy solder are also available ready-mixed with borax in syringe form. When working with gold, the same color and karat of solder must be used. Roll solder down with a rolling mill to produce really thin strips to help during the pallion-cutting process.

REVERSE-ACTION TWEEZERS: Available with curved and straight ends, these steel tweezers operate under tension and are used to hold pieces together during soldering. Avoid holding tubing as the tube walls can collapse during heating.

THIRD HAND: Reverse-action tweezers can be screwed into these adaptable bases to allow workpieces to be held at any angle.

SOLDERING PICK OR PROBE: An alternative to soldering tweezers, these steel tips with a wooden handle can be dunked in borax before picking up and placing a pallion of solder on the workpiece.

SAFETY PICKLE OR ACID: Once a workpiece has cooled, it must be put in the pickle to remove the oxides formed from heat. Never throw hot work into solution as it could splash.

PICKLE CONTAINERS: Expensive units can be bought from jewelry suppliers. However, slow cookers or a pyrex dish with a lid on an electric ring at a low setting will do the same thing. Keep the pickle warm (maximum 122°F/50°C), but never boiling.

SURGICAL-STEEL SOLDERING TWEEZERS: Good quality tweezers used for picking up solder pallions and moving things during soldering.

SOLDERING TURNTABLE: Allows the workpiece to be turned and viewed from all angles during soldering. Also useful for annealing.

TEMPORARY PROTECTORS OF JOINS: Rouge powder mixed with oil or water to form a paste, heat insulating gel known as Thermogel, or white-out correction fluid can all be used. Remove after heating with pickle or white spirit.

BRASS, WOODEN, OR PLASTIC TWEEZERS: Used to immerse and remove workpieces from pickle. Rinse thoroughly in water before touching. A sieve with a plastic or brass (not steel) mesh is good for containing jewelry in the pickle.

STONESETTING TOOLS

SETTERS CEMENT: Becomes temporarily soft when warmed. The workpiece is put in and the cement hardens to hold it in place. The cement is then gently warmed again to remove the jewelry. Excess cement can be removed with lighter fluid, cellulose thinners, or alcohol.

CLAW-SETTING TOOL: Similar to a cabochon-setting tool, but with a D-shaped groove in the face to house a claw and prevent the tool from slipping when setting a stone.

BEZEL ROLLER: Curved-edge tool with a wooden handle. When used with a rocking action, the steel face smooths metal over stones.

RING CLAMP: Holds a ring or workpiece securely while working on detail or setting a stone.

CABOCHON-SETTING TOOL: Flat-faced steel tool with round wooden handle to push metal over stones.

BURNISHING TOOL: Available curved or straight with a wooden handle, this tool smooths metal over stones and adds polished finish details to small areas. Also available made from agate, bone, or plastic.

PIN VISE: Fine detail and small adjustments can be achieved by hand by securing a drill bit or stonesetting burr in a pin vise. Supplied with different-sized chucks.

COLLET PLATE AND PUNCHES:
Conical punch and conical cutouts in plate produce collets of different depths and angles. Available with 17-degree or 28-degree angles and various shapes: round, oval, hexagonal, square, rectangular, emerald, and pear-cut.

GRAINING TOOLS: Steel tools that fit into a wooden handle and have concave polished hemispherical cutouts in the tip. Used to secure and round-off grains and the tips of claws when gently rocked in a circular motion. Available in sets of different sizes.

GYPSY-SETTING TOOLS: Specially-adapted steel tools whose tips have been shaped, emery papered, and polished into smooth, rounded tips. Masonry nails are good for this. Create two, one less pointed than the other, for best results.

GRAVERS: Used to engrave designs and patterns, as well as creating grooves, raising grains, and carving mounts for stones. They need to be adapted to the correct length and inserted into a wooden handle before use. Available in various profiles (see illustrations at right).

OILSTONE OR SHARPENING STONE:
A double-sided carborundum stone with one medium and one fine side. When combined with machine oil, it is used for sharpening gravers, drill bits, etc.

GRAVERS

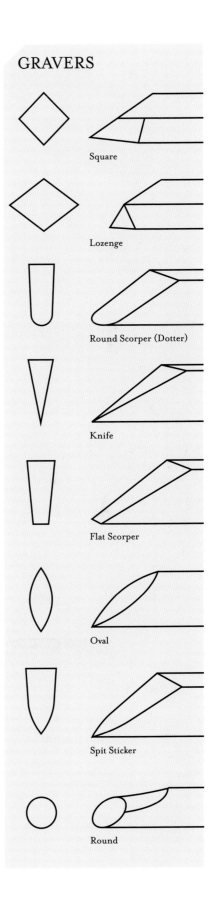

Square

Lozenge

Round Scorper (Dotter)

Knife

Flat Scorper

Oval

Spit Sticker

Round

ELECTRICAL EQUIPMENT

BENCH DRILL: Used for drilling and enlarging holes and seating stones. Always ensure the chuck key is removed before activating the motor. Mark the metal first with a scribe and a hide mallet, and wear safety goggles.

BARREL POLISHER OR TUMBLER: Jewelry is placed inside the polisher with stainless steel shot of different sizes and shapes and a powdered soap called Barrelbrite and water tumbles in a revolving container on a motorized spindle to give a polished finish. Great for chains and textured surfaces, the shot can be replaced with ceramic cutting cones and water to produce a matte finish.

PENDANT MOTOR: A suspended dentist's drill activated by a foot pedal to give varying speeds and leave both hands free to guide the shaft and hold the workpiece. Can do everything the bench drill, barrel polisher, and bench polisher can, plus much more, such as rapid emery papering.

BENCH POLISHING MOTOR: Has two rotating spindles at either side to which mops can be attached to be used in conjunction with polish (usually tripoli first, followed by rouge) to create a smooth, shiny finish, or more abrasive wheels for a satin finish.

ULTRASONIC: Creates tiny bubbles when ultrasonic sound waves are passed through a soapy liquid to remove dirt and polish.

BURRS

BEARING CUTTER OR HART BURR: Steel burr with teeth or blades used to cut grooves and remove small amounts of metal.

CUP BURR: Similar to graining tools, these burrs have spherical concave cutout ends with blades that can remove metal and finish the tip of a claw.

CONE-SHAPED BURR: Conical-shaped burrs of different sizes with blades to remove tiny areas of metal and make small adjustments.

SETTING BURR: Similar to a bearing cutter, but straight sided at the top of its profile. The blades create a "seat" for a stone, mimicking the shape of its underside or pavilion.

CYLINDER BURR: This straight-sided cylindrical burr has diagonal blades that can remove metal.

BUD BURR: Shaped like a bud, this steel tool is similar to a ball burr as its blades can cut a spherical shape for a stone to sit in. Versatile as it has both a spherical area and a pointed area.

BALL BURR: Spherical steel burr with teeth or blades, can be used at any angle to cut out a "cup" for a stone to sit in.

WHEEL BURR: Similar to a cylinder burr, but wider and shorter. Teeth or blades run vertically.

FLAME BURR: Similar to a bud burr, but longer and thinner. Used for working on small details and areas to help seat a stone.

WIRE WRAPPING

BEADING MAT: Rectangular felt mat designed to stop beads rolling.

OPTICAL AIDS

LOUPE: Small single lens used to detect faults, cracks, or characteristics in a stone. Use x10 magnification.

EYEGLASS: Single lenses of different magnifications that can be held in the eye, leaving both hands free.

OPTIVISOR: Head-mounted lenses of different strengths with directional lights attached.

MICRO PAVE

ENGRAVER'S BALL: Holds workpieces securely to allow access from all angles.

MICROSCOPE: High powered lenses used to show jewelry in great detail.

MICROMOTOR: Precise motor, electronically balanced to ensure minimum vibration. Can be foot-pedal operated or set at certain speeds.

PNEUMATIC ENGRAVER: Operates with compressed air to give a pump action of precise, even pressure. Hand held, variable speeds.

GLUE

Glueing should be avoided where possible. The best glue is usually a two-part epoxy that needs to be mixed together in equal quantities. It has an elasticity that is less snappable and more hard wearing than superglue.

PEARL STRINGING

BEADING SILK: Twisted silk of various colors and thicknesses.

BEAD REAMER: Diamond-tipped conical tool used to increase the size of a hole through a bead.

FRENCH WIRE OR GIMP: Thin coil of wire that can be cut to desired length and protect beading silk near to a clasp from wear.

CLEAR NAIL VARNISH OR SUPERGLUE: For reinforcing the short end of beading silk on a workpiece.

BEAD KNOTTING TOOL: Tool with sprung point and handle to ensure tight knots.

PRECIOUS METAL CLAY

NONPOROUS SURFACE: Use laminated paper or a glass, ceramic, or teflon tile for rolling PMC.

PLAYING CARDS: For determining depth of PMC.

ROLLERS: Plastic tubing works well for rolling out PMC.

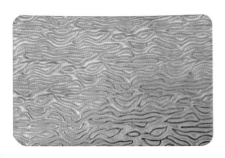

PLASTIC OR BRASS TEXTURE SHEETS: To impress textures into metal clay. Available from PMC suppliers.

OLIVE OIL OR NONPETROLEUM-BASED LUBRICANT: To act as a release.

NEEDLE TOOL OR DRESS-MAKING PINS: For marking PMC.

STENCILS AND COOKIE CUTTERS: For creating outlines.

SCALPEL BLADE AND HANDLE: For cutting PMC.

PLASTIC WRAP: For keeping unused PMC moist.

TWEEZERS, DRINKING STRAWS, COCKTAIL STICKS, Q-TIPS: For shaping, rolling, texturing, and smoothing PMC.

SILVER PASTE AND A PAINTBRUSH: For repairing, smoothing, and adding patches to PMC.

TORCH: For firing PMC.

DIGITAL KITCHEN TIMER: For timing the firing.

EMERY BOARD OR SANDING PAD: For smoothing the edges and surfaces of PMC.

RUBBER BLOCK: For resting the workpiece on for easy access from all angles.

POLISHING PAPERS: To create a smooth finish. Available in various grades.

FOOD DEHYDRATOR: For drying out PMC before firing. Optional.

ENAMELING KILN: For firing PMC. Optional; a jeweler's torch is a good equivalent.

CHAPTER 2
CHOOSING STONES

STONE TYPES

OPPOSITE
PAGE

*Ring series by
Jantje Fleischhut.
Amethysts and
topaz are cut
through lengthwise
and set in
14K gold.*

NATURAL STONES

These are made either of solid crystalline masses of mined minerals or organic substances. Some gemstones are formed deep under the earth's surface, some closer to the crust, and others are affected by conditions above ground. They vary hugely in color, density, clarity, shape, size, and value.

LABORATORY GROWN OR SYNTHETIC STONES

The mineral makeup of these stones is the same as natural stones, but they are grown in a laboratory under intense heat and pressure to mimic the conditions underneath the earth's surface. Lab-grown gems have the same chemical and physical characteristics as natural stones, but they are cheaper and do not have any inclusions.

SIMULATED STONES

These are also grown in a laboratory, but are not made up of minerals. They are designed to imitate the look of a real stone but differ completely in characteristics such as hardness, color, and clarity.

CRYSTAL TYPES AND STRUCTURES

A gemstone is cut depending on its crystalline internal structure and its symmetry. Crystals fall into seven structural groups: cubic, tetragonal, orthorhombic, trigonal, monoclinic, triclinic, and hexagonal.

There are two lines of symmetry that affect a cut: mirror symmetry (an imaginary mirror through the center of the crystal) and axis of symmetry (an imaginary line running vertically through the crystal so that if it were rotated it would appear the same two, three, four, or six times during a rotation).

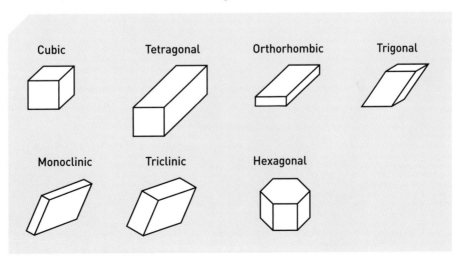

Cubic   Tetragonal   Orthorhombic   Trigonal

Monoclinic   Triclinic   Hexagonal

LAPIDARY

Lapidary is the process of cutting, polishing, and engraving gems to specific shapes and styles. The magical process of transforming a rough piece of rock into a well-cut gem occurs as follows:

1. Taking structure and symmetry into account, a diamond-tipped rotating wheel is used to begin cutting facets.

2. Preforming maximizes the weight and beauty of the finished piece and minimizes wastage. This stage is often performed on a rotating steel wheel.

3. Shaping involves more accurate and detailed application of facets. The stone is held at set distances against a hand-operated wheel.

4. Polishing is usually completed on a steel wheel with diamond paste to reveal the character and individuality of the piece.

CABOCHON CUTS

A cabochon cut has a smooth, flat, or curved top and a flat base. Both opaque and translucent stones are used for this style, and it is usually polished. The cabochon shape is often carved into cameos, and it lends itself well to optical effects such as cat's eyes and star stones.

Less expensive materials such as turquoise, lapis lazuli, amethyst, and hematite are often cut in a cabochon shape, and can be great for learning the basics of stonesetting.

Although usually flat on the underside, cabochon profiles can vary from a straight-faced slice or slab to a low, shallow dome or a higher curve. The shape of the base can be round, oval, square, rectangular, triangular, or cushion cut.

CUT NAME	SIDE VIEW
LOW DOME	
HIGH DOME	
CONE	
BULLET	
DOUBLE BEVELED	
HOLLOW/CARBUNCLE	
DOUBLE	
FLAT CUT/SLAB	
BUFF TOP	
BUFF TOP (CROSS-VAULTED)	

FACETED CUTS

A faceted stone has faces cut into the surface and a pointed underside. Transparent and translucent stones are most popularly used for these cuts, and the facets are marked out so that light is reflected back and forth inside the stone. Factors such as weight and the locations of flaws affect the positions of these facets.

The round, brilliant-cut style, originally designed for the ideal diamond shape, has a traditional format of 57 cuts to ensure that these stones appear proportionally uniform regardless of their size.

There are many amazing variations and combinations of these cutting methods designed to show off a stone to its best advantage. A selection are shown on pages 33–34.

THIS PAGE

Green tourmaline set in 18K yellow gold and rhodolite garnet set in stainless steel. Rings by Michael Berger.

FACET TERMINOLOGY

CROWN VIEW

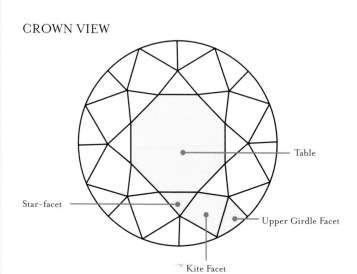

Table

Star-facet

Upper Girdle Facet

Kite Facet

SIDE VIEW

Girdle Diameter

Table Size

Crown Angle

Girdle

Crown Height

Pavilion Angle

Pavilion Height

PAVILION VIEW

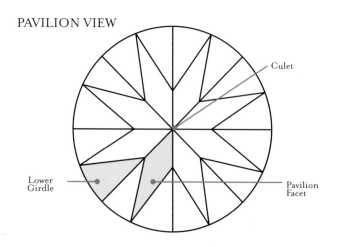

Culet

Lower Girdle

Pavilion Facet

CUT NAME	CROWN VIEW
FANCY	
OVAL	
TRILLIANT OR TRILLION	
PEAR	
PENDELOQUE	

CUT NAME	CROWN VIEW
MARQUISE	
CUSHION	
ROSE	
BUFF-TOP	
BRIOLETTE	

CUT NAME	CROWN VIEW		CUT NAME	CROWN VIEW
PRINCESS			BAGUETTE	
HEART			SQUARE	
CONCAVE			EMERALD	
MIRROR			OCTAGON	
STEP			CROSS AND FRENCH	

THIS PAGE

Top: Orange
spessartine garnet
set in 14K yellow
gold. Ring by
Will White.

Bottom: Sterling-
silver earrings with
faceted pale-blue
quartz stones. By
Zoe Harding.

CHARACTERISTICS OF STONES

A well-cut stone shows even color, does not include too many inclusions, and has good brilliance. It should also retain its qualities, be durable, and resistant to cracking and scratching.

COLOR: Bright and rich colors that absorb light well make a stone attractive. Some have an even color distribution, and others exhibit different colors.

CUT: An appropriate number of facets compared with stone size is important. Most of the carat weight should be visible when viewed from the top. Cabochon cuts should be smooth and symmetrical.

CARAT: This measurement is used when weighing gemstones. A carat is divided into 100 "points" of 2mg each, so one carat equals 200mg. Weights are given to the nearest point or $\frac{1}{100}$ of a carat, so for example, a 50 point stone can be described as half a carat. Generally, the bigger the stone the more expensive the carat price.

CLARITY: The transparency of a stone. Gemstones include tiny fissures known as inclusions that can affect the overall look of the piece. Inclusions can lower the value of a stone, but they can sometimes enhance a piece. Fissures can increase the fragility of a stone, so check that your stones can endure the setting process.

LUSTER: The quality of the polished surface and the effect of light as it is reflected back off the surface of a stone. Generally, the harder the stone, the higher the polish.

BRILLIANCE: The effect an evenly and well-cut gem has on the reflection of light in its interior. Ineffective facets will allow light through to the back of the stone instead of keeping it inside. Fire or dispersion is produced when white light is split into the separate colors of the spectrum and these are deflected back at different angles so the individual shades become visible.

OPTICAL EFFECTS: A lot of gems fall into the catagory of macro crystalline (crystals visible to the naked eye), but some are cryptocrystalline (made up of tiny structures only visible through a microscope). Light refraction within a stone, or its refractive index (RI), can be measured with a refractometer. The following are the result of these formations influencing light to create beautiful phenomena:

Iridescence and the play of color: These are due to the movement of light within cleavage breaks and layers in a stone. In some stones, the full spectrum will be seen, but in others only some colors are visible.

Asterism: This star effect is seen predominantly in cabochon stones and common displays show a four- or six-pointed star. A well-cut gem will have long inclusions and exhibit a sharp, centralized star.

Chatoyancy (cat's eye effect): Creates an illusion of a single line like that of a cat's eye within a cabochon stone. Also created by long, thin inclusions.

Color change: This can happen when a stone is viewed under two different types of light (for instance in sunlight, then artificial light).

Pleochroism: The ability of a stone to appear to possess slightly different colors when held at different angles.

Aventurescence: A sparkling, glitter-like appearance.

Adularescence: A bluey, milky appearance.

Silk: The smooth, even, and uniform spread of light.

SPECIFIC GRAVITY OR RELATIVE DENSITY: The process of weighing a stone relative to the equivalent weight of the same volume of water.

CLEAVAGE: Gemstones have three-dimensional crystalline structures, the atoms of which can be held together in different formats, therefore they can have lines along which they can break more easily.

FRACTURE: Can occur as a result of too much pressure during setting, overheating and rapid cooling, or a split caused over time by an inappropriate setting.

AUTHENTICITY: Some gems are treated with heat, dyes, bleach, oils, or irradiation. If purchasing a very expensive stone, ensure a certificate, clear receipt, and returns policy are provided to establish authenticity and proof of purchase.

DURABILITY: Created in 1812 by Friedrich Mohs, the Mohs Hardness Scale charts minerals according to their hardness or "scratchability." With talc at number 1.00 and the softest (it can be scratched by all the other minerals) and diamond at number 10.00 and the hardest (it cannot be scratched by any of the other minerals), it is a very useful resource when choosing which stone is suitable for which setting (see chart at right).

MOHS HARDNESS	MINERAL USED FOR COMPARISON
10.00	Diamond
9.00	Ruby, Sapphire
8.00	Aquamarine, Emerald, Spinel, Topaz
7.00	Amethyst, Citrine, Garnet, Iolite, Kunzite, Peridot, Tanzanite, Tourmaline, Zircon
6.00	Diopside, Lapis lazuli, Orthoclase, Turquoise
5.00	Obsidian
4.00	Coral, Fluorite
3.00	Pearl
2.00	Amber
1.00	Talc

POPULAR MINERALS AND ORGANICS

AMBER

Made from fossilized tree resin. Amber is used in perfume, is said to possess healing properties, and can contain plant debris, small animals, and insects from millions of years ago. Popular cuts are cabochons, cameos, or beads to exhibit the interior to the full. These lovely organics look amazing when set in yellow or rose gold.

PROVENANCE: Russia, USA, Italy, Dominican Republic, Burma, Romania

COLOR: Pale and golden yellow to dark brown and even blue and green

FAMILY: Organics

CRYSTAL GROUP: Amorphous

HARDNESS: 2.00–3.00

REFRACTIVE INDEX: 1.54

SPECIFIC GRAVITY: 1.05–1.10

CONSIDERATIONS: Sensitive to sunlight, hot water, perfume, and hairspray. Take care when setting and store separately to other jewelry to avoid scratching.

JET

This black, opaque stone is made up of carbon derived from coal and fossilized wood. When highly polished it can be used as a mirror, and some types can have stones set into it. Best known in cabochon, cameo, and flat, polished forms.

PROVENANCE: UK, France, Germany, Russia, Spain, Turkey, USA, Portugal

COLOR: Black

FAMILY: Organics

CRYSTAL GROUP: Amorphous

HARDNESS: 2.00–4.00

REFRACTIVE INDEX: 1.66

SPECIFIC GRAVITY: 1.30–1.35

CONSIDERATIONS: There are convincing imitations on the market: real jet feels warm to the touch. Store in a damp cloth to prevent it drying out or cracking.

CORAL

The skeletons of marine invertebrates called polyps, made of calcium carbonate, assemble together and build up into reefs over thousands of years to form coral. This opaque, soft material is easily carved and cut into cabochons, cameos, and beads.

PROVENANCE: Italy, France, Hawaii, Australia, Japan, West Indies, Malaysia, Algeria, Tunisia

COLOR: Orange, red, dark red, pink, blue, black, white

FAMILY: Organics

HARDNESS: 2.50–3.50

REFRACTIVE INDEX: N/a

SPECIFIC GRAVITY: N/a

CONSIDERATIONS: Can be pierced, filed, emery papered, and polished. Drill underwater with a diamond-tipped drill bit. Avoid excess pressure when setting. Will fade over time. Clean with warm water and a cloth; avoid chemicals and acids.

PEARL

Formed from layers of the mineral argonite, a calcium carbonate secreted by the mantle of a living shelled bivalved mollusk when an irritant is implanted inside its shell. Pearls are categorized as either natural or cultivated, and either fresh water or sea water.

PROVENANCE: Australia, China, Indonesia, Japan, Philippines, Tahiti, Red Sea, Cook Islands, New Zealand, Mexico, Korea

COLOR: White, cream, black, gold, pink, orange, silver, yellow

FAMILY: Organics

CRYSTAL GROUP: N/a

HARDNESS: 3.00–4.00

REFRACTIVE INDEX: 1.53–1.68

SPECIFIC GRAVITY: 2.60–2.78

CONSIDERATIONS: Avoid contact with perfumes, hairspray, cosmetics, chlorine, ammonia, or excessive perspiration. To store, wipe gently with a warm, damp towel, wrap in acid-free tissue, and keep in a soft, dark-colored cloth pouch.

SHELL

Types of shell used for jewelry include abalone, paua, conch, helmet, and large pearl oyster shells. Can be cut into a cabochon or cameo, or polished and used in inlay.

PROVENANCE: China, Japan, Australia, USA, New Zealand, Africa

COLOR: Peach, pink, black, white, brown, multicolored

FAMILY: Organics

HARDNESS: 3.00–4.50

REFRACTIVE INDEX: 1.52–1.65

SPECIFIC GRAVITY: 2.60–2.80

CONSIDERATIONS: Straightforward to pierce, emery paper, file, and polish. Drill under water with a diamond-tipped drill bit. Keep away from chemicals, acids, and excessive heat.

MALACHITE

This secondary copper mineral has opaque light and dark green stripes or bands making each cabochon-cut stone or bead unique, some of them reminiscent of woodgrain.

PROVENANCE: Namibia, Tanzania, Zambia, Australia, UK, France, Germany, Israel, Russia, USA

COLOR: Pale green to near-black strips

FAMILY: Malachite

CRYSTAL GROUP: Monoclinic

HARDNESS: 3.50–4.00

REFRACTIVE INDEX: 1.85

SPECIFIC GRAVITY: 3.90–4.00

CONSIDERATIONS: Lends itself well to carving and smooth surfaces. Keep away from chemicals.

FLUORITE

Has bicolor and multicolor banding and a glassy luster. It has a fluorescence and some examples have a color change. Can be cut in a variety of styles from step and cushion to cameo.

PROVENANCE: India, Brazil, UK, Russia, France, Germany, Italy, Norway, Pakistan, USA, Czech Republic

COLOR: Clear, blue, purple, pink, red, yellow, black, etc. Crosses the entire spectrum

FAMILY: Fluorite

CRYSTAL GROUP: Cubic

HARDNESS: 4.00

REFRACTIVE INDEX: 1.43

SPECIFIC GRAVITY: 3.2

CONSIDERATIONS: Usually too soft to be faceted, take care when setting and tumbling. Ensure it is adequately supported from the reverse.

DIOPSIDE

Produced by crystals of square or eight-sided cross-sections, often twinned and having a perfect cleavage in two directions. It can range from translucent to opaque and exhibits pleochroism.

PROVENANCE: Canada, Germany, Italy, India, Russia, Sweden, USA, Pakistan, Sri Lanka

COLOR: Green, white, clear, blue, brown, gray, purple

FAMILY: Pyroxene

CRYSTAL GROUP: Monoclinic

HARDNESS: 5.00–6.00

REFRACTIVE INDEX: 1.66–1.72

SPECIFIC GRAVITY: 3.20–3.60

CONSIDERATIONS: Stones are usually small. Winter months can hamper mining in Russia, making supply sporadic and prices fluctuate. An excellent green looks great set in white metal.

LAPIS LAZULI

Constructed of contact metamorphosed limestone containing lazurite and calcite, this gorgeous rock is blue with flecks of sparkling, gold-colored pyrite, and white calcite. It is quite soft, so is usually cut as cabochons or cameos, and is also used as an inlay material.

PROVENANCE: Afghanistan, Pakistan, Burma, Canada, Italy, Russia, USA, Angola

COLOR: Ultramarine, azure blue

FAMILY: Lazurite

CRYSTAL GROUP: Cubic

HARDNESS: 5.00–6.00

REFRACTIVE INDEX: 1.50

SPECIFIC GRAVITY: 2.50–3.00

CONSIDERATIONS: Avoid ultrasonics or steam cleaning; a natural, unpolished finish is beautiful.

OBSIDIAN

Semitranslucent pieces of this natural glass are step cut, while opaque stones are fashioned into cabochons. Snowflake obsidian exhibits white flecks caused by the internal inclusion of potassium feldspar.

PROVENANCE: Mexico, USA, Ecuador, UK, Hungary, Iceland, Russia, Japan, Italy, New Zealand, Armenia, Slovakia, Guatemala

COLOR: Clear, black, dark green, gray, brown, occasionally red

FAMILY: Obsidian

CRYSTAL GROUP: Amorphous

HARDNESS: 5.00–6.00

REFRACTIVE INDEX: 1.48–1.53

SPECIFIC GRAVITY: 2.33–2.60

CONSIDERATIONS: Easily scratched and cracked.

TURQUOISE

An opaque hydrated phosphate of copper and aluminum with streaks and patches of black limonite and black manganese oxide. Turquoise is usually bead, cameo, and cabochon cut, although rare translucent examples do also exist. Partners well with silver, both in affordability and hardness.

PROVENANCE: Afghanistan, China, India, Iran, USA, Australia, Chile, Egypt, Mexico, Russia, Tibet

COLOR: Pale blue, blue green, greenish-gray

FAMILY: Turquoise

CRYSTAL GROUP: Triclinic

HARDNESS: 5.00–6.00

REFRACTIVE INDEX: 1.61–1.65

SPECIFIC GRAVITY: 2.60–2.80

CONSIDERATIONS: Good for practicing cabochon setting, but be wary of corners chipping and damage to veins. Avoid heat, tumbling, acids, and chemicals. Soaks up creams and oils.

HEMATITE

This blood-colored mineral can be cut into beads, cabochons, and cameos, as well as brilliant and table cuts. Its opaque, metallic, shiny appearance gives it a feeling of density and solidity.

PROVENANCE: Ascension Island, Australia, UK, Italy, Mexico, Norway, Switzerland, USA, Venezuela

COLOR: Dense black, gunmetal, red

FAMILY: Haematite

CRYSTAL GROUP: Trigonal

HARDNESS: 5.00–6.50

REFRACTIVE INDEX: 2.94–3.22

SPECIFIC GRAVITY: 4.90–5.30

CONSIDERATIONS: Lends itself well to carving, but can chip. Keep separate from acids and chemicals.

MOLDAVITE OR TEKTITE

These amazing stones are small pieces of natural glass formed by meteors hitting planet earth, then melting and combining with rock. They are only found in a few areas and their markings are usually either "splash form" or "layered."

PROVENANCE: Australia, China, Austria, Czech Republic, Germany, Laos, Malaysia, Philippines, Thailand, Vietnam, Ivory Coast, Libya

COLOR: Black and green

FAMILY: Tektite

CRYSTAL GROUP: Amorphous

HARDNESS: 5.50–6.50

REFRACTIVE INDEX: 1.48–1.50

SPECIFIC GRAVITY: 5.50–6.50

CONSIDERATIONS: Dark or bottle green is most suitable for faceting, but uncut moldavites are more valuable and attractive.

OPAL

An opal's play of color has flashes of a rainbow-like appearance caused by faults in the pyramid-shaped framework of silicon oxide, which is scattered internally with water. It is amorphous (has no crystal structure) and can be formed as huge fissures within host rocks, also known as "potches" or "matrices," after which the opal can be named. For example, the Black Opal has a dark background color as a result of its potch. Other types of opal include: Boulder Opal, Fire Opal, Green Opal, Jelly Opal, Peruvian Opal, Semi Black Opal, White Opal, Water Opal, and Wood Opal. Can be cut into step and cabochon.

PROVENANCE: Predominantly Australia. Also Brazil, Czech Republic, Italy, Romania, South Africa, Ethiopia, Peru, Indonesia, Zimbabwe

COLOR: Many. Clear, opalescent white, red, brown, gray, blue, green, black, etc.

FAMILY: Opal

CRYSTAL GROUP: Amorphous

HARDNESS: 5.50–6.50

REFRACTIVE INDEX: 1.33–1.46

SPECIFIC GRAVITY: 1.80–2.30

CONSIDERATIONS: Can dry out if mined too quickly, cracking horizontally. Avoid drilling, excess pressure during setting, and exposure to chemicals, cosmetics, and creams.

LABRADORITE

Relatively clear, this very distinctive stone is related to plagioclase feldspar and is rich in sodium. It has metallic reflections known as schiller that create the appearance of rainbow reflections when held at a certain angle. Often cut as cabochons or a flat polished surface.

PROVENANCE: Canada, China, India, Madagascar, Australia, Finland, Germany, Russia, USA, Costa Rica, Mexico

COLOR: Clear, gray, yellow, orange, red, smoky black

FAMILY: Feldspar

CRYSTAL GROUP: Triclinic

HARDNESS: 6.00–6.50

REFRACTIVE INDEX: 1.55–1.57

SPECIFIC GRAVITY: 2.70–2.72

CONSIDERATIONS: Difficult to cut and can have cracks. Beads can cause damage if rubbed against each other.

MOONSTONE

These stones are a variety of orthoclase and exhibit a bluey-white, milky opalescence, which is caused by the intergrowth of two types of feldspar creating a layered effect. Moonstones are often cut into cabochon or cushion styles. The higher the dome, the more effective the adularescence.

PROVENANCE: Sri Lanka, Australia, Brazil, Burma, India, Mexico, Norway, Madagascar, USA

COLOR: Clear, brown, gray, blue, pink, yellow, rainbow

FAMILY: Feldspar

CRYSTAL GROUP: Monoclinic

HARDNESS: 6.00–6.50

REFRACTIVE INDEX: 1.51–1.57

SPECIFIC GRAVITY: 2.56–2.62

CONSIDERATIONS: Great for learning cabochon setting, its glass-like quality is complemented by silver, but be wary of horizontal cracking.

SUNSTONE

Related to labradorite, amazonite, and moonstone, small copper or pyrite inclusions present in this stone give it a twinkling effect. Sunstone can be faceted or cabochon cut and can exhibit pleochroism.

PROVENANCE: Madagascar, India, Tibet, USA, Canada, Norway, Russia

COLOR: Red, orange, yellow

FAMILY: Feldspar

CRYSTAL GROUP: Triclinic

HARDNESS: 6.00–6.50

REFRACTIVE INDEX: 1.53–1.55

SPECIFIC GRAVITY: 2.56–2.65

CONSIDERATIONS: The stunning glitter effect is well set off in a claw setting. Most feldspars are composed of two cleavages, so take care when setting. Avoid chemicals, excessive heat, and rubbing against other stones.

ORTHOCLASE

A potassium feldspar type, orthoclase are affordable and have good clarity. They can sometimes twin, and have almost straight cleavage faces. Often found in granites and syenites, several varieties of orthoclase are cut as gemstones to offer different colors. The presence of iron gives yellow orthoclase its shades. Some types have a similar appearance to moonstone and labradorite.

PROVENANCE: Australia, Burma, Germany, India, Italy, Mexico, Madagascar, Switzerland, USA, Sri Lanka

COLOR: Yellow, off-white, pink, red, orange, brown

FAMILY: Feldspar

CRYSTAL GROUP: Monoclinic

HARDNESS (MOHS SCALE): 6.00–6.50

REFRACTIVE INDEX: 1.51–1.54

SPECIFIC GRAVITY: 2.55–2.58

CONSIDERATIONS: Often step cut as it tends to be quite fragile. Avoid knocks and chemicals.

KUNZITE

This durable pink stone exhibits phosphorescence (a glow that continues in a darkened space after exposure to sunlight) and pleochroism. Best seen in a faceted stone in a channel, claw, or almost backless setting.

PROVENANCE: Brazil, Afghanistan, Pakistan, Madagascar

COLOR: Pinks, lavender, lilac, yellow

FAMILY: Spodumene

CRYSTAL GROUP: Monoclinic

HARDNESS: 6.00–7.00

REFRACTIVE INDEX: 1.65–1.68

SPECIFIC GRAVITY: 3.16–3.20

CONSIDERATIONS: Fades in prolonged exposure to sunlight. Susceptible to knocks.

BLOODSTONE, OR HELIOTROPE

So called as it exhibits small red spots resembling blood, this stone is quite soft, so is often cut into cabochons, cameos, and beads. Traditionally worn in signet rings.

PROVENANCE: USA, Australia, Brazil, China, Czech Republic, Germany, India, Italy

COLOR: Greens and blues with spots of red

FAMILY: Chalcedony Agate

CRYSTAL GROUP: Trigonal

HARDNESS: 6.50

REFRACTIVE INDEX: 1.54

SPECIFIC GRAVITY: 2.59–2.61

CONSIDERATIONS: Avoid excess pressure when setting.

CHRYSOPRASE

The opaque color should be uniform throughout in this stone and is so intense that a dyed or treated replica can be very convincing. Cuts vary from cabochon, cameo, and bead to rose. Chrysoprase is a fantastic all-rounder: durable, with an even texture, affordable in lower grade colors, and flattering to other stones.

PROVENANCE: Australia, USA, Brazil, Germany, Russia, South Africa, Czech Republic, Tanzania

COLOR: Yellow to fresh apple greens. Sometimes mistaken for jade.

FAMILY: Chalcedony Quartz

CRYSTAL GROUP: Trigonal

HARDNESS: 6.50

REFRACTIVE INDEX: 1.54

SPECIFIC GRAVITY: 2.58–2.64

CONSIDERATIONS: Colors can fade in sunlight or heat.

JASPER

The mixture of chalcedony, opal, and quartz gives jasper its unique qualities of structure and color. It is opaque and lends itself well to cabochon and cameo cuts, as well as being used in mosaics.

PROVENANCE: Australia, Chile, India, Madagascar, Mexico, Libya, USA, Sweden, UK, Iceland, Iran, Ukraine

COLOR: Red and yellow (created by iron oxide), brown or green with spots or gray stripes

FAMILY: Chalcedony Agate and Quartz

CRYSTAL GROUP: Trigonal

HARDNESS: 6.50–7.00

REFRACTIVE INDEX: 1.54

SPECIFIC GRAVITY: 2.59–2.61

CONSIDERATIONS: Looks great when set in silver or gold. Avoid barrel polishing.

NEPHRITE JADE

Also known as jadeite and nephrite, these are in fact two different minerals, but are often found near to each other. Formed of interlinked crystals made dense under high pressure, this material is immensely tough and is often used to make tools, weapons, and cutting implements. Usually cut in cabochon, bead, and cameo form. The more expensive the stone, the more vivid, bright, and pure the color.

PROVENANCE: China, Burma, Canada, Mexico, Russia, USA

COLOR: Usually green, also blue, brown, cream, lavender, white, and yellow

FAMILY: Jade

CRYSTAL GROUP: Monoclinic

HARDNESS: 6.50–7.00

REFRACTIVE INDEX: 1.61–1.68

SPECIFIC GRAVITY: 2.90–3.36

CONSIDERATIONS: Strong, but can be brittle. Often dyed, but these can usually be easily detected.

PERIDOT

This gem is "idiochromatic," meaning that iron, the coloring element, is actually part of the crystal, so peridots are always green. It is a variety of olivine, has a velvety appearance, and looks fantastic as a faceted cut.

PROVENANCE: Canada, Egypt, Burma, Norway, Pakistan, USA, South Africa, Tanzania, China

COLOR: Yellow green, olive green

FAMILY: Olivine

CRYSTAL GROUP: Orthorhombic

HARDNESS: 6.50–7.00

REFRACTIVE INDEX: 1.64–1.69

SPECIFIC GRAVITY: 3.27–3.37

CONSIDERATIONS: Exhibit step, baguette, and cushion cuts in a minimal setting to display the stone well. Avoid household chemicals, overheating, and acids. Clean with a toothbrush, mild detergent, and warm water.

TANZANITE

An excellent example of pleochroism, tanzanite exhibits a large amount of different hues when viewed from different directions and under different lights, from pure indigo blue under daylight to pinky violets under incandescent light. Tanzanite is heat-treated to enhance these colors. Can be used as a convincing replica for sapphire.

PROVENANCE: Tanzania

COLOR: Blues, violet, indigo, lilac

FAMILY: Zoisite

CRYSTAL GROUP: Orthorhombic

HARDNESS: 6.50–7.00

REFRACTIVE INDEX: 1.68–1.70

SPECIFIC GRAVITY: 3.35

CONSIDERATIONS: Avoid excessive heat or extreme changes in temperature. Chips easily—wear on special occasions only.

GARNET

This is a family of more than 10 stones that share a similar crystal structure, but differ slightly in color, density, and refractive index. The red color is the most familiar. Both faceted and cabochon cut garnets are good for practicing stonesetting techniques with, as they are affordable and quite hard.

PROVENANCE: Kenya, Madagascar, Mali, Namibia, Nigeria, Russia, Sri Lanka, Tanzania

COLOR: Various: red, green, yellow, orange, violet, brown

FAMILY: Garnet

CRYSTAL GROUP: Orthorhombic

HARDNESS: 6.50–7.50

REFRACTIVE INDEX: 1.70–1.89

SPECIFIC GRAVITY: 3.51–4.16

CONSIDERATIONS: Sometimes brittle, so take care not to crack the girdle when setting.

CITRINE

This bright yellow stone is so colored by the addition of iron. It can be cut into brilliant, cabochon, and pendeloque styles. Natural citrine is quite rare, but it can be produced synthetically by heat-treating amethyst.

PROVENANCE: Brazil, USA, France, Russia, Madagascar, Mozambique, Tanzania

COLOR: Yellows and oranges

FAMILY: Quartz

CRYSTAL GROUP: Trigonal

HARDNESS: 7.00

REFRACTIVE INDEX: 1.50

SPECIFIC GRAVITY: 2.60–2.70

CONSIDERATIONS: Sensitive to excessive heat or light.

QUARTZ

Members of this family are found in many places globally and within many rock types. Quartz can be bought in a multitude of colors and shapes. It is categorized in two groups: crystalline (large, recognizable crystals, including amethyst, ametrine, citrine, green amethyst, rose quartz, rutilated quartz, rainbow quartz, smoky quartz, and tiger's eye) and cryptocrystalline (consisting of crystals that are too small to be easily told apart and including agate, carnelian, sard, chrysophase, jasper, onyx, and bloodstone). Looks beautiful as cabochon, faceted, or bead cuts.

PROVENANCE: South Africa, Tanzania, Mozambique, Madagascar, Brazil, worldwide

COLOR: Many. Clear, pink, blue, green, yellow

FAMILY: Quartz

CRYSTAL GROUP: Trigonal

HARDNESS: 7.00

REFRACTIVE INDEX: 1.50

SPECIFIC GRAVITY: 2.60–2.71

CONSIDERATIONS: Uncut stones can also create stunning pieces of jewelry. Resilient to pressure during setting, but avoid direct sunlight as colors can fade.

IOLITE

Although usually violet, iolites are pleochroic gems, which is especially noticeable when they are set in earrings or necklaces with light coming through the setting. Can be cut into step cuts, cabochons, bullet cuts, and mixed cuts.

PROVENANCE: India, Madagascar, Sri Lanka, Bolivia, Brazil, Canada, Germany, Sweden, USA, Burma (Myanmar), Finland

COLOR: Violet blue, light blue, yellow gray in the same stone

FAMILY: Cordierite

CRYSTAL GROUP: Orthorhombic

HARDNESS: 7.00–7.50

REFRACTIVE INDEX: 1.50

SPECIFIC GRAVITY: 2.53–2.65

CONSIDERATIONS: Be careful to avoid chipping when setting.

TOURMALINE

Because of their structure and large size, this group of crystals are often cut in long rectangular shapes and are not greatly bountiful. They occur in granite pegmatic veins and get their distinctive color arrangements from the presence of the mineral elbaite. Cut into facets, cabochons, steps, and slices, they display pleochroism, multicolors, and occasionally chatoyancy. The group also includes green, indicolite, paraiba, and rubelite tourmalines.

PROVENANCE: Brazil, Kenya, Madagascar, Malawi, Mozambique, Nigeria, Sri Lanka, Tanzania, Russia, USA

COLOR: Green, pink, near black, pale blue, dark blue

FAMILY: Tourmaline

CRYSTAL GROUP: Conchoidal

HARDNESS: 7.00–7.50

REFRACTIVE INDEX: 1.62–1.64

SPECIFIC GRAVITY: 3.01–3.20

CONSIDERATIONS: Be wary of fractures, especially in multicolored stones. Avoid knocks and clean regularly with a mild detergent, soft toothbrush, and warm water.

EMERALD

Its unique color, hardness, slow growth, and rarity makes this stone one of the most beautiful, desirable, and valuable in the world. Although durable, emeralds can crack when under pressure or given a harsh blow; the emerald cut was designed to be sympathetic to the stone's structure during cutting and setting. Transparent pieces are usually faceted and more translucent stones are usually made into cabochons and beads.

PROVENANCE: Brazil, Colombia, Pakistan, Siberia, Zambia, Zimbabwe, USA, Australia, India, Russia, Afghanistan

COLOR: Green

FAMILY: Beryl

CRYSTAL GROUP: Prismatic

HARDNESS: 7.00–8.00

REFRACTIVE INDEX: 1.57–1.58

SPECIFIC GRAVITY: 2.67–2.78

CONSIDERATIONS: Avoid chemicals that can affect the oil or wax that are sometimes added to fissures to disguise them and enhance the color. Do not let the stone get knocked.

AMETHYST

This stone is often set in silver and is available in both cabochon and faceted cuts, as well as beads. The purple hues are caused by the addition of iron, a multicolored amethyst can display a range of colors from deep purple to clear.

PROVENANCE: Madagascar, Kenya, Brazil, Uruguay, Zambia, Australia, Canada, India, Germany, USA

COLOR: Violet, purple, clear

FAMILY: Quartz

CRYSTAL GROUP: Trigonal

HARDNESS: 7.00

SPECIFIC GRAVITY: 6.50

REFRACTIVE INDEX: 1.54–1.55

CONSIDERATIONS: Avoid excess pressure when setting, especially in a weaker area. Good for bezel-setting practice.

ZIRCON

Exhibits dispersion (light entering the stone is separated into a prism) and birefringence (light is split in two ways). It has an adamantine (diamond-like) luster. The zircon cut, containing eight more facets to the pavilion than the round brilliant cut, was invented to enhance these qualities. Often used as a diamond substitute.

PROVENANCE: Cambodia, Nigeria, Sri Lanka, Tanzania, Australia, Brazil, Burma, Norway, Russia, Thailand, USA, Vietnam

COLOR: Clear, light brown, red brown, gray, blue, green, yellow

FAMILY: Zircon

CRYSTAL GROUP: Tetragonal

HARDNESS: 7.50

REFRACTIVE INDEX: 1.93–1.98

SPECIFIC DENSITY: 4.60–4.70

CONSIDERATIONS: Hard but brittle, so can chip. Avoid heat, ultrasonic cleaning, and ultraviolet light.

AQUAMARINE

Iron adds color to this stone to produce beautiful sea-like shades. Available in cabochon, brilliant, step cuts, and beads. Has a glass-like quality.

PROVENANCE: Brazil, Madagascar, Mozambique, Namibia, Nigeria, Tanzania, Zambia, Pakistan

COLOR: Blue, turquoise, green

FAMILY: Beryl

CRYSTAL GROUP: Hexagonal

HARDNESS: 7.50–8.00

REFRACTIVE INDEX: 1.57–1.59

SPECIFIC GRAVITY: 2.68–2.80

CONSIDERATIONS: Do not overheat or exert excess pressure when setting

HELIDOR

A yellowish-green stone, created by some of the aluminum in the crystal structure being replaced by iron, the more intense the color, the more frequent the inclusions. Characteristics include perfect, six-sided, prismatic hexagonal crystals; they can be cut into baguette, marquise, and table cuts, among others. Cabochon stones can exhibit chatoyancy or asterism. It is very difficult to mine similar pieces of helidor, so although popular, it is often only used in unique, commissioned pieces.

PROVENANCE: Brazil, Madagascar, Namibia, Nigeria, Russia, USA

COLOR: Yellows, orange-yellow, green

FAMILY: Beryl

CRYSTAL GROUP: Hexagonal

HARDNESS: 7.50–8.00

REFRACTIVE INDEX: 1.57–1.60

SPECIFIC GRAVITY: 2.80

CONSIDERATIONS: Can have oils added or may have been heat treated, so be wary of them coming into contact with chemicals.

SPINEL

Pure spinel is white, but the addition of impurities produces many other colors. These hard gemstones are often faceted, but are also available in cabochons. When well cut, their lively color intensity is displayed to the full.

PROVENANCE: Madagascar, Tanzania, Vietnam, Afghanistan, Australia, Pakistan, Russia, Sweden, Turkey, USA, Burma (Myanmar)

COLOR: Various: red, brown, black, green, blue

FAMILY: Spinel

CRYSTAL GROUP: Cubic

HARDNESS: 8.00

REFRACTIVE INDEX: 1.71–1.72

SPECIFIC GRAVITY: 3.60

CONSIDERATIONS: Looks good set in silver and white or yellow gold. Avoid acids and chemicals if inclusions are present.

TOPAZ

This hardest of silicate minerals is mined from both alluvial mines and host rocks. Most well-known for its blue and yellow colors, topaz can be faceted and cabochon cut, faceted beads being especially beautiful. Step cuts display subtle colors well. A colorless topaz can be mistaken for a diamond.

PROVENANCE: Brazil, Mozambique, Nigeria, Russia, Australia, Japan, Mexico, Sri Lanka, Sweden, Ukraine, USA, Norway, Pakistan

COLOR: Clear, pale yellow, blue, green, pink, sherry brown, orange

FAMILY: Topaz

CRYSTAL GROUP: Orthorhombic

HARDNESS: 8.00

REFRACTIVE INDEX: 1.60–1.63

SPECIFIC GRAVITY: 3.50–3.60

CONSIDERATIONS: Quite durable, but avoid chemicals, polishing, and knocks. A sherry-brown stone looks great set in yellow gold.

RUBY

Rubies consist of corundum and are given their red intensity by the presence of chromium, among other elements. They exhibit fluorescence, asterism, and pleochroism. They can be faceted or cut into cabochons. Almost as hard as diamonds, rubies can be rarer and more expensive, but convincing synthetics are available.

PROVENANCE: India, Kenya, Madagascar, Sri Lanka, Tanzania, Thailand, Vietnam, Afghanistan, Australia, Cambodia, USA

COLOR: Brownish/pinkish/purplish red, red

FAMILY: Corundum

CRYSTAL GROUP: Trigonal

HARDNESS: 9.00

REFRACTIVE INDEX: 1.76–1.77

SPECIFIC GRAVITY: 3.90–4.10

CONSIDERATIONS: These resilient stones lend themselves well to everyday wear and look wonderful set in yellow gold. Although they have no cleavage, there are many tiny flaws that can cause weak points. Will not be affected by heat or ultrasonic, but check settings periodically for wear.

SAPPHIRE

Sapphires include any corundum gem that is not red. They are allochromatic, acquiring their colors from the trace elements iron and titanium, among others. They can be faceted or cut into cabochons; they can exhibit asterism and, rarely, color change. Sapphires are often heat treated or irridated to improve their color and clarity, and these treatments are permanent.

PROVENANCE: India, Pakistan, Sri Lanka, Australia, Cambodia, China, Kenya, Madagascar, Nigeria, Tanzania, Thailand, Vietnam, USA, Burma (Myanmar)

COLOR: Blue, clear, pink, yellow, green, red, purple, black

FAMILY: Corundum

CRYSTAL GROUP: Trigonal

HARDNESS: 9.00

REFRACTIVE INDEX: 1.76–1.77

SPECIFIC GRAVITY: 3.90–4.10

CONSIDERATIONS: Ideal for everyday wear, sapphires can be cleaned in an ultrasonic. Check settings periodically.

DIAMOND

Gem dealers and jewelers rely on the "four Cs": cut, color, clarity, and carat weight when choosing a diamond; an ethically-sound origin should also be taken into account. The round brilliant is a very recognizable cut, but diamonds are cut in many other styles such as marquise, cushion, baguette, and pendeloque. The diamond grading system was developed by the GIA (Gemological Institute of America) and consists of a Diamond Clarity Scale and a Diamond Color Scale.

GIA DIAMOND CLARITY SCALE

(FL) FLAWLESS: Shows no inclusions or blemishes under the 10x magnification of a jeweler's loupe.

(IF) INTERNALLY FLAWLESS: Has no inclusions under 10x magnification, but has some surface blemishes.

(VVS1 AND VVS2) VERY, VERY SLIGHTLY INCLUDED: Contains tiny inclusions that are difficult to see under 10x magnification.

(VS1 AND VS2) VERY SLIGHTLY INCLUDED: Contains tiny inclusions of different structures underneath 10x magnification.

(SI1, SI2, AND SI3) SLIGHTLY INCLUDED: Contains inclusions of different structures under 10x magnification to an experienced grader.

(I1, I2, I3) INCLUDED: Contains obvious inclusions under 10x magnification.

(PK) PIQUE: Contains inclusions easily visible without a loupe.

GIA DIAMOND COLOR SCALE

D, E, F: Stones with pure tints and rare colors.

G, H, I: Can offer good value as they seem of the same quality as D, E, and F colors to the untrained eye.

J, K, L: Very faint yellow tints. Good value.

M–Z: Diamonds outside the usual color range are known as "fancy" and include red, green, yellow, brown, black, blue, etc.

Some diamonds are "treated" with heat, replicating the conditions found in nature, to enhance their colors.

PROVENANCE: Africa, India, Russia, Brazil, Borneo, China, Canada, Sierra Leone, Namibia, Tanzania, Australia

COLOR: According to the GIA Diamond Color Scale

FAMILY: Carbon

CRYSTAL GROUP: Cubic

HARDNESS: 10.00

REFRACTIVE INDEX: 2.41

RELATIVE DENSITY: 3.50

CONSIDERATIONS: Keep separate to other stones to avoid scratching. Protect from heat when soldering, be careful of weak points when setting, and keep clean with warm water, a mild detergent, and soft toothbrush.

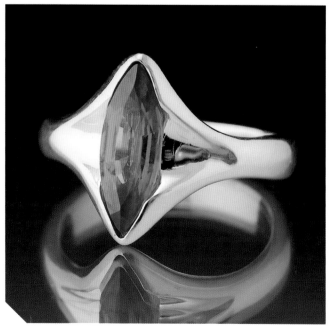

SELECTING A STONE

OPPOSITE
PAGE

Top: Large
segmented
neckpiece with
hand-carved
perspex and
metallic elements
by Emmeline
Hastings.

Bottom left: Orange
sapphire set
in sterling
silver. Ring by
Konstanze Klaus.

Bottom right: Purple
amethyst set
in sterling
silver. Ring by
Konstanze Klaus.

THIS PAGE

Peridot, pink
topaz, and smokey
quartz set in
sterling silver.
Pendant by
Zoe Harding.

This can be an exciting and pleasurable process, and after experience is gained, your confidence in decision-making will quickly grow.

Ensure that the necessary paperwork for certificated stones will be produced.

Use a 10x magnification loupe to examine the stone in detail. Observe its qualities under both artificial light and daylight. Take an example of the metal it will be set in to ensure a sympathetic match. The dealer will place it on a black or white background and turn it with tweezers to give you a better look.

If in doubt, do not remove the stone from its box—it will usually have to be paid for if it is dropped or cracked.

Be clear about your budget and requirements, but feel free to ask for advice—the dealers I have bought stones from have always been friendly, knowledgeable, and helpful.

A faceted stone should have evenly cut faces, an attractive color or colors, and no obvious flaws. A hard stone can be set in a hard metal to prevent the setting weakening and becoming loose during wear; soft stones should be set in softer metals so that they don't crack during setting or from pressure when set.

Select a cabochon carefully: check that the underside is truely flat, otherwise it could rock in its setting. Make sure there are no vulnerable or crumbly areas on the surface, and that the corners do not crack during setting or wear.

A cabochon stone that is smaller than $\frac{5}{16}$in (8mm) in diameter can be fiddly to work with for a beginner, and a low stone can be just as tricky to set properly as a high-cut piece.

METALS FOR STONESETTING

It is useful to practice with base metals such as copper, brass, and nickel silver (also known as German Silver) as these are much cheaper than precious metals, but share similar properties. Most tool shops stock sheet, rod, and wire in base metals.

Precious metals can be bought in various forms, including sheets, tubing, wire, rod, discs, ready-made components, bezel strip, gallery strip, chain, and casting grain.

The format, thickness, height, and length must be specified when buying precious metal. Prices fluctuate from day to day depending on the market value. Ready-priced offcuts of precious metals can be bought on request—these cannot be cut down, but are slightly discounted.

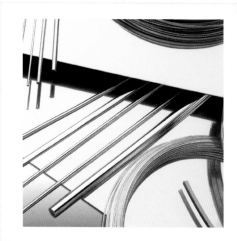

GOLD

Gold is malleable and ductile. It is naturally yellow in color and, in its purest form (24K) is usually too soft to work with, but when mixed with various alloys it is given different colors and karats that make it more durable and affect the way the gold behaves when worked. The higher the karat, the more malleable the metal. White gold is an alloy of gold and either nickel, manganese, or palladium. Red or rose gold is an alloy of gold and copper. Green gold is an alloy of gold and silver. Gray gold is created by the addition of silver, manganese, and copper. Different alloys are appropriate for different stonesetting processes, for example, yellow-gold bezel strip is very pure and soft, so is used for cabochon setting, whereas white gold in 9K or 18K is harder, so is more suitable for channel or pave setting.

SILVER

Silver is available in various alloys. With 99.9% purity, fine silver is very soft and malleable, making its uses limited. It is used for bezel strip as an option for setting cabochons, and does not tarnish, oxidize, or produce firestain as no copper or other alloys are present. Britannia silver is 95.8% silver and 4.2% copper. A popular and versatile alloy, sterling silver is 92.5% pure silver with the addition of 7.5% copper. Its malleability and strength is ideal for most fabrication and stonesetting, but it can tarnish and produce firestain. Argentium silver was created in 1996, and was designed to reduce firestain during the fabrication and casting processes by replacing some of the copper content with germanium.

PLATINUM

Platinum is a precious, hard, dense, malleable, and ductile metal that is versatile and ideal for holding a variety of gemstones. It is a steely, gunmetal gray color, and has a very high melting point. Other members of the platinum group are palladium, rhodium, ruthenium, iridium, and osmium.

PALLADIUM

Another popular metal for jewelry making and stonesetting, palladium was discovered in 1803 and has enjoyed a revival in recent years as it is a little cheaper than platinum with a similar appearance, varying from tin white to yellowy white

PLATING

Jewelry can be plated with layers, or microns, of various gold colors and karats. Rhodium, a member of the platinum family, will plate to give a white, reflective, scratch-free surface.

SETTINGS & TECHNIQUES

CHAPTER 3
BASIC FABRICATION & FINISHING TECHNIQUES

Before we get started with stonesetting tutorials, this chapter will provide an overview of the basic fabrication and finishing techniques you'll need to use in your jewelry making.

MEASURING AND CUTTING METAL

Work out the dimensions of your piece on paper before scribing them onto metal, or stick a more intricate design down onto the surface.

The most accurate and versatile method of cutting is to use a piercing-saw frame with a saw blade housed under tension. As a general rule, there should be three teeth to the thickness of the sheet worked on. Check the teeth are running smoothly down toward the handle and that the blade is taut by placing the top of the piercing-saw frame into the V of the bench peg, tightening the top of the blade into the top nut, and pushing into the frame with your hand or shoulder to temporarily reduce the distance between the nuts in the frame while tightening the bottom nut. The blade should "ping" when twanged with a finger tip when the frame is released—if that tension is not felt, the blade may snap during use.

Hold the workpiece firmly against the benchpeg and use the saw upright in your dominant hand to create long, slow strokes using the whole length of the blade, adding beeswax to act as a lubricant. Keep your body fully facing the bench, the dominant hand and arm firm yet relaxed, try not to push forward too heavily on the blade, and avoid any sharp turns to the left or right.

See page 16 for more information about cutting tools.

FILING

Large areas can be filed using a hand file with a wooden handle attached. The file's teeth are most effective on the away stroke, and, when filing straight edges, it is important not to let the file arc during the stroke as a bowed outline will appear.

Support the piece on the bench peg, watch the tip of the file throughout the stroke, and check straight edges with an engineer's square. When matching two pieces of metal to each other, work on one side first until it is completely true, then start matching the other one to it without altering the first.

See page 19 for more information about filing tools.

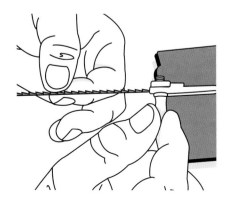

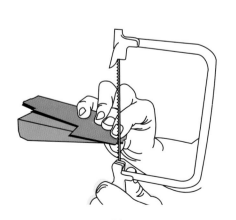

ANNEALING

Annealing is the process of heating metal to a specific temperature to make it pliable and flexible before texturing or forming.

When you're annealing, you need to keep a close eye on the metal, so follow either of these setups:

a. Prop the metal against a firebrick at a slant—this allows you to be at eye level with the workpiece, encourages the heat to travel around the metal, and prevents the firebrick drawing too much heat away.

b. Hold the metal upright in reverse-action tweezers. Some of the heat will be drawn away from the metal through the tweezers, so the piece might take slightly longer to heat up. Annealing at this angle prevents a torch head becoming blocked or damaged.

Before you start, turn off any strong directional lights. The torch's flame should be bushy and appropriately sized, with a dark blue outer flame and a pale blue internal cone. The tip of this pale blue area should touch the surface of the metal throughout the process. Hold the torch still, and observe the metal change from a dirty ocher color, quickly followed by oil and petroleum-like hues of greens, blues, purples, and sometimes reds, followed by a black tide, and then a magical sunset glow. Once this final color is achieved (a dull red in the case of silver and gold, orange-yellow for platinum, and yellow-orange held for 30–60 seconds for palladium) the whole piece needs to be evenly annealed by moving the flame slowly across the surface of the metal at this temperature until it is equally softened throughout.

Some jewelers quench metal in water when it has cooled to a black heat and some air cool in case rapid heat loss could put stress back into the piece. Placing the annealed metal onto a steel block using tweezers helps to speed up the air cooling process.

Once the metal is completely cold, carefully immerse it in safety pickle for a couple of minutes to remove any oxides from the surface.

PICKLING

Pickling cleans metal that has been heated to remove any dirt or oxides. Pickle is a weak acid and water solution—originally a one-part sulfuric acid, nine parts water ratio—and is now bought in a dry granule form known as safety pickle. Mix and dispose of safety pickle according to manufacturers' guidelines and use a sieve or tweezers to lower the cooled metal into the solution while wearing an apron and safety goggles. Leave for a couple of minutes (longer in the case of stubborn borax deposits), rinse thoroughly before touching the piece, and then dry.

Use only plastic sieves and brass, wooden, or plastic tweezers with pickle: anything made of steel has a copper plating reaction with the solution that leaves a pink deposit on silver or gold. This discoloration can be removed with heat, emery paper, wire wool, and pumice powder, and once the offending steel is removed, the pickle solution can usually be reused. See page 21 for information about pickling equipment.

Pickle alternatives include a warm solution of lemon juice, vinegar, or citric acid diluted with water.

TEXTURING AND FORMING

TEXTURING WITH METAL HAMMERS

Put annealed metal on a steel block to ensure equal pressure is exerted from above and below. Experiment with hammers that vary in size and shape. See how the shapes differ as the pressure used per stroke and space between the marks alters.

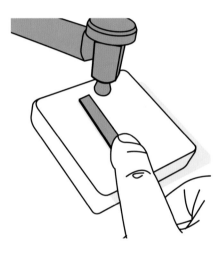

BURRS IN THE PENDANT MOTOR

Attach a stone-setting burr, such as a small bearing cutter or flame burr, into the pendant motor and use it like an engraving tool. If the angle of the burr is low and used like a pen, it can be used to "draw" onto the surface of the metal.

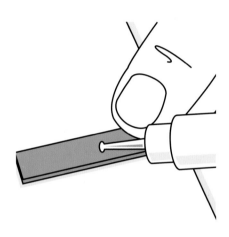

ROLLERPRINTING

This technique involves selecting dry, crisp materials of a hard texture and passing them through a rolling mill with annealed metal to impress their profile onto the metal's surface. Items such as dried leaf skeletons, wire, lace, emery paper, and watercolor paper all leave beautifully detailed impressions.

Place a piece of scotch tape with the sticky side uppermost on a tabletop and attach the texturing items using tweezers. Turn the tape over, stick this arrangement onto flat metal, and wrap it up in a little newspaper to make it easier to hold and to prevent the metal from distorting too much during the rolling process. Adjust the width of the rollers by turning the wheel on the top of the mill until rolling the workpiece requires a little effort, but not extreme force. Rolling two or three times, each time bringing the rollers a touch closer together, creates a deeper effect.

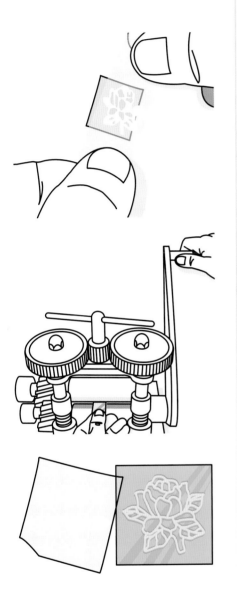

DRILLING HOLES

Make an indentation with a scribe and a hide mallet. Place the metal on some wood, activate the motor if using an electrical drill, and carefully lower the drill bit into the metal. If the bit bows, you're exerting too much pressure. Use a lubricant, remove the drill bit from the metal from time to time to prevent overheating, and keep going until wood shavings appear through the hole.

DAPPING

Put an annealed disc in a recess in the dapping block that is larger than the disc, hold a dapping punch vertically that fits in the chosen concave disc, and strike the punch from above using a hide mallet. Continue, using gradually smaller disc sizes and punches until the desired size and depth of dome is achieved.

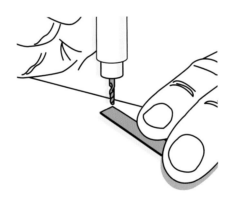

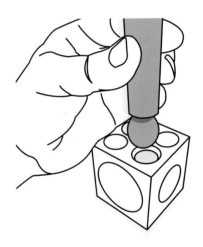

SOLDERING

Silver solder is made up of silver, copper, and zinc, and usually comes in three grades: hard, medium, and easy (hard enameling solder and extra easy solder are also available). These different grades become molten at different temperatures with hard solder running at the highest, then medium solder, followed by easy solder. The amount of zinc governs the temperature at which solder will flow, so if there are multiple joins in a piece, complete the first join using hard solder, then medium solder for the next join, followed by easy solder. This process protects any previous joins from popping open. If there is only one join in a piece of work, use hard solder. See pages 20–21 for information about soldering tools, and page 182 for solder melt temperatures.

Cut up some tiny pieces or "pallions" of solder using tin snips. Put these on a firebrick close to the workpiece.

Use stainless steel soldering tweezers to pick up the pallions. Rest the piece on the pallions and use the heat from the torch to encourage the solder to flow in an upward direction.

Once the workpiece has resettled and the borax has become black and sticky (now is a good time to add some solder if not already present as it adheres to the sticky, warm borax with ease), it is time to focus the heat on the seam. Tilt the flame down toward the solder, then slowly and evenly, keeping the tip of the pale blue part of the flame on the surface of the metal, trace a line of heat up through the seam. When it's molten, solder is attracted toward the heat source, so it is important to heat both sides of the join to the same temperature to avoid the solder bleeding to the left or right. If this straight line of heat is repeated slowly and confidently (try not to let the flame leave the workpiece), the solder will form a ball and shoot up to the seam creating a thin silver line.

Check there are no gaps in the join by holding it up to the light (if light comes through, the seam must be opened, refiled, and brought back together again). Use a paintbrush to apply borax or flux to the inside and outside of a join to keep that area of the metal clean and free of oxides—solder cannot run across dirty metal.

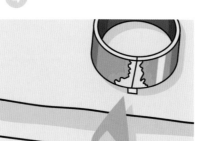

Heat the piece gently and slowly until it is evenly warmed, trying not to let the flame get trapped inside an enclosed area as this causes overheating. At this point, the borax bubbles and evaporates, which might cause movement: have the tweezers in your dominant hand to stabilize the workpiece if necessary.

FINISHING TECHNIQUES

EMERY PAPERS

After the surface has been prepared with a file, it needs to be worked on with emery paper. Both emery and wet and dry papers range in coarseness, the best results obtained when used in sequence from the coarsest to the finest.

Start mid-range—grade 400 or 600—and work over the piece, trying to keep the emery paper moving in the same direction as the file marks until the major scratches have been removed. Next, move on to a grade 800, followed by 1,000, then 1,200, finishing with 2,000. The more effort and attention to detail that is paid at this stage, the far superior the finish will be; any further polishing will not remove any scratches, but will merely make them appear deeper and more visible.

POLISHING

Textures, chains, earrings, and pieces with areas that are difficult to reach can be finished in a barrel polisher.

Flat, mirror finishes can be achieved using a polishing motor. These motors are used in two stages; an abrasive polish called tripoli with a calico mop prepares the metal before the final buff performed with a fine polish known as rouge is applied using a soft cotton mop. These mops revolve quickly, so hold the workpiece in both hands, keep it to the lower section of the mop, and turn the machine off if the piece gets snatched away (once the spindle has stopped revolving, the work can be retrieved from the dust hood behind).

Miniature mops can be used with a pendant motor for polishing small areas. The pendant motor is foot-pedal operated, so you have both hands free to hold and turn the piece while polishing.

SATIN AND MATTE FINISHES

These finishes tend to be deeper and more effective when applied to a surface that has already been polished. There are many products on the market that will achieve these finishes, including pumice powder (used with a toothbrush and water), wire wool, ceramic chips and water in place of stainless steel shot in the barrel polisher, Scotch-Brite, glass brush, brass brush, rubber and carborundum burrs, Garyflex abrasive blocks, and emery papers. Each product produces a subtly different effect, so experiment with several to find which you prefer.

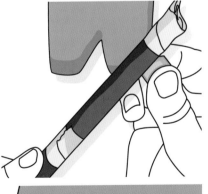

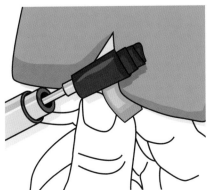

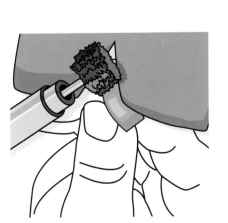

CHAPTER 4
PRONG & SNAP SETTING

Prong settings are ready-made settings that can house a range of gemstone shapes. They are widely used within recycled jewelry and are a convenient method of resetting unusual cuts, such as those found in vintage pieces. The findings are sometimes already attached and the pieces have a polished finish.

They are available as a basic setting style and also as pendants, hook-and-stud earrings, and charm attachments for bracelets. Prong settings are ideal for beginners to gain experience of holding workpieces and exerting the correct pressure during stonesetting.

SNAP SETTINGS

These are a quick and versatile alternative to prong settings, and are widely available for use with round stones, as well as other shapes. They are more suitable for using with faceted stones rather than cabochons, as they house the pointed underside better.

STONES AND METALS

Faceted stones and cubic ziroconias are good to practice with. Prong settings are usually produced in silver, gold, or platinum.

PRONG SETTING WITH A FACETED OR CABOCHON STONE

SKILL LEVEL

Beginner

WHAT YOU NEED

- Faceted or cabochon stone
- Ready-made prong setting
- Soldering equipment
- Finishing and polishing tools
- Snipe-nose pliers
- Setters cement (optional)
- Butane lighter fluid or cellulose thinners
- Bearing cutter or triangular needle file
- Setting tool (claw or flat faced)

1 Choose a stone that sits level in the setting and is a good fit: for a faceted stone, the culet should not extend through the base of the setting and the prongs should not extend over and disguise too much of the stone.

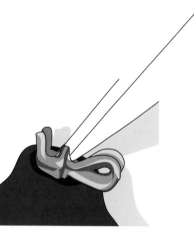

2 For small settings, warm up some setters cement with a cool, bushy flame until it is soft but not bubbling. Insert the workpiece using soldering tweezers so that it is secure, of even depth, and not too buried. Rings with a finished setting soldered on can be held in a ring clamp.

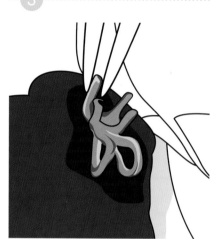

3 Use snipe-nose pliers to slightly open each prong by an equal amount, see how the stone sits, then repeat. Do not manipulate the prongs too much as they can become weak.

4 If you're using a faceted stone, you can cut a slight ledge or groove onto the inside of each claw using a triangular needle file or bearing cutter to house the girdle, but ensure that this indent does not exceed half the thickness of the prong as it could snap during setting. Insert the stone.

PRO TIP

Don't press too hard on the prongs as the pushing tool can slip, scratch the metal, chip or break the stone, or set the stone at an uneven angle.

⑤

There are usually four prongs on a setting: push the prongs over the stone using snipe-nose pliers, bending diagonally opposite prongs to secure the stone. Position the pliers toward the base of each prong, then press forward and down.

Alternatively, you can use a claw-setting tool. Use the bench peg as a back rest and push in and down on each prong from the front in turn (effectively pushing from the front and back of the piece at the same time so the stone is being clamped into place). Rotate the piece as you work until the stone is secure.

⑥

Warm the cement briefly and very gently with a soft, small bushy flame, remove the piece, and clean off any wax residue using butane lighter fluid or thinners. Remove any small marks with a fine polishing paper, followed by a burnishing tool.

SNAP SETTING TUTORIAL

Upturn the stone onto a flat surface. Push the setting down in a vertical position onto the back of the stone. As even pressure is applied from above, the claws are forced to widen slightly as they slide down the pavilion, then, as they grasp the girdle, the stone "snaps" into place.

①

②

③

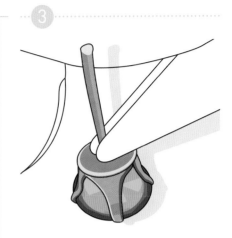

④

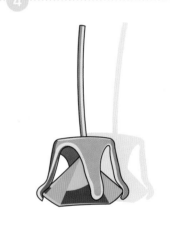

⑤

GALLERY

OPPOSITE PAGE

Top: Prong-set diamonds in rose gold. Earrings by Jennifer Briggs Jenkins.

Bottom left: Prong-set citrine ring by Lucie Veilleux.

Bottom right: Prong-set diamonds, blue sapphires, and tsavorite garnets. Rings by Jennifer Briggs Jenkins.

THIS PAGE

Top left: Prong-set blue topaz pendant by Patrick Irla.

Top right: Prong-set topaz ring by Scott A. Fowler.

Bottom left: Prong-set rough yellow sapphire, with asymmetrically-set citrines and yellow sapphires. Ring by Anna Bario and Page Neal. Setting by Anthony Fontana.

Bottom right: Lemon quartz stone held in four "paw" prongs. Ring by Konstanze Klaus.

CHAPTER 5
PRECIOUS METAL CLAY

OPPOSITE
PAGE
Simulated ruby
flush-set into
fine silver PMC.
Pendant by
Janice Heaton.

Precious Metal Clay (PMC), also known as Art Clay Silver (ACS), consists of metal powder mixed with an organic binder that burns away during firing to leave a 99.9% metal purity. It can be modeled, molded, rolled, and textured before firing.

Findings, settings, and stones are pushed into the clay before it is fired. PMC shrinks during firing by between 3% and 12%, partly due to water evaporating from the clay. The thickness of the workpiece (determined by the number of playing cards stacked on either side of the clay when it's rolled out) needs to exceed the depth of the stone to be set, and it is best to keep the immediate area surrounding the setting free of texture to avoid damage to the pattern when embedding the setting or stone. It is important to work quite quickly as the clay can dry out: create a model in Blu-tack first to establish the texture, dimensions, and order of work, and ensure that your tools are clean, oiled, and ready for use.

STONES AND METALS

Any stones above 7.00 on the hardness scale are suitable. Any man-made, laboratory-created, and most synthetic stones can be fired, although be wary of doublets, which have two layers so can easily split. Clear cubic zirconias are a great choice, although their colors can change slightly. Test-fire stones by wrapping them in ceramic fiber blanket and firing them in a kiln. Gemstones that can't be fired can be set in a PMC piece after firing. PMC is fine silver when fired, so can be soldered to base metals, sterling silver, and gold.

SETTING A CABOCHON STONE INTO PRECIOUS METAL CLAY

SKILL LEVEL

Beginner/Intermediate

WHAT YOU NEED

- Cabochon stone
- Bezel strip and pencil
- Piercing saw, tin snips, or scissors
- Round or oval triblets
- Precious Metal Clay
- Nonporous surface (laminated paper, a glass or ceramic tile)
- Playing cards
- Roller (plastic tubing)
- Texture sheets
- Olive oil
- Needle tool, dress making pin, a stencil and scalpel, or cookie cutters
- Plastic wrap
- Tweezers
- Drinking straw
- Cocktail sticks
- Food dehydrator or electric hot plate
- Silver paste and a paintbrush
- Kiln
- Ceramic fiber blanket
- Flat needle file
- Emery board or sanding pad
- Brass brush or polishing papers
- Wire for spacer
- Setting tool
- Burnisher

Choose a stone and bezel strip that are complementary to each other. The bezel strip needs to be at least three quarters of the height of the stone at this stage.

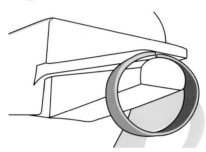

Wrap the bezel strip around the base of the stone. Mark the strip and cut it using a piercing saw, scissors, or tin snips, then shape it to fit the stone using round-nose pliers, D-shape pliers, or a round or oval triblet. The ends of the bezel strip need to butt up against each other so that it forms a close fit around the stone when placed flat on the tabletop. Use a flat needle file to straighten the sides of the join. Check the fit by turning the stone and bezel strip upside down. If you're using an oval stone, ensure that the seam is on a long length.

Lubricate and set up a pile of eight playing cards either side of a texture sheet on top of a nonporous surface. Lightly smear your tools and hands with olive oil.

Firmly and with even pressure, begin to roll out the clay to an eight card thickness. Roll in one direction, then turn by 90 degrees and roll again to achieve an even thickness. Reduce the stack height to a six-card thickness on either side of the clay, cover with a top texture plate, and roll again.

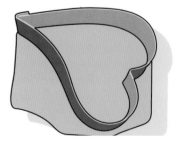

When both the front and back of the piece are decorated, gently place the workpiece on a lightly greased playing card and create the outline using a needle tool and stencil, a sharp scalpel, or a cookie cutter. Wrap any excess clay immediately in plastic wrap.

VARIANT SETTING

Gallery strip and paper clay create lovely wrap-around settings as an alternative to bezel strip. For an oval stone, ensure the wrap-around detail lies on a long side of the setting.

6

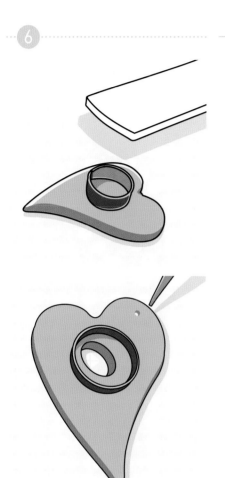

Push the bezel strip in to a depth of around ²/₃₂in (1mm), ensuring that the top edge is horizontal and the seam does not open. Create a smaller hole for light to pass through the stone when it is set using a drinking straw or small, shaped cutter, followed by a cocktail stick to make a pilot hole for a jump ring to pass through to suspend the piece from.

7

Leave the piece in a food dehydrator for 10 to 15 minutes or on an electric hot plate on the lowest setting for one minute.

8

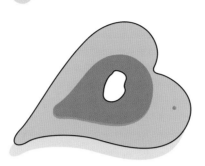

After drying, turn the piece over to check where the layer of reinforcement should be: usually the bezel strip will have created a faint impression where it has been pushed into the clay. Choose a cookie cutter that is slightly larger than the area to be covered and roll out the clay to a two-card thickness. Cut out the shape, paint the reverse with a thin layer of silver paste, and adhere it to the underside of the setting, not forgetting to create a hole through this layer in the same way as step 6.

9

Using a cocktail stick or very thin paintbrush, build up thin layers of silver paste along the seam in the bezel strip and the join where it connects to the workpiece. Don't let the paste bleed into the surrounding texture.

10

Fire the piece in a kiln at 1,650°F (900°C) for two hours (no preheating is required). Use a ceramic fiber blanket or vermiculite to hold the pieces level while they are in the kiln. After firing, leave the piece to air cool or quench it in water.

11

File the silver paste around the join in the bezel strip with a needle file, then create a smooth texture around the edges using either a medium-grade sanding pad or an emery board. Follow with a brass brush and soapy water for a matte finish, or polishing papers for a shiny finish. If the bezel strip is too tall, insert a thin wire jump ring inside the setting to raise the stone up and keep it level.

12

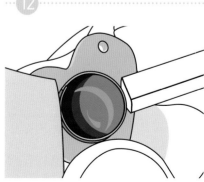

Use a setting tool to set the stone. Rest the back of the setting against the benchpeg and push from the front to secure the north, south, east, and west points. Tuck the bezel strip around the stone and finish with a burnisher.

CLAW SETTING INTO PRECIOUS METAL CLAY

SKILL LEVEL

Beginner/Intermediate

WHAT YOU NEED

- Precious Metal Clay or Art Clay Silver
- Round faceted stone
- Ready-made claw setting
- Olive oil
- Nonporous surface
- Playing cards
- Roller
- Texture sheets
- Cookie cutters
- Plastic wrap
- Silver paste and paintbrush
- Tweezers
- Cocktail stick
- Food dehydrator (optional)
- Sanding pad or emery board
- Rubber block
- Pin vise
- Drill bit
- Brass brush
- Polishing papers
- Claw-setting tool

Oil the nonporous surface, playing cards, texture sheets, your hands, and the roller. Choose a claw setting that is deep enough to be held in place by the fired clay without it being too tall.

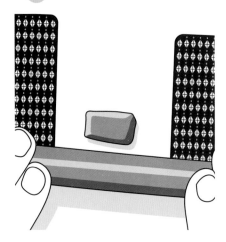

Place a texture sheet down on the nonporous surface, texture side uppermost, followed by a stack of four cards on either side of the texture sheet. Roll the clay to the required thickness. Place a top texture sheet on the clay and roll it again. Cut out two shapes with the cookie cutters, one small and one large.

Place the two cutout shapes on an oiled playing card. Paint silver paste or water onto the reverse of the smaller piece, then adhere the two pieces together.

Use tweezers to place the setting and push it levelly down so that the top of the first gallery is flush with the clay. If the top textured layer curls, use a little water and a paintbrush to gently push it back into place.

5

Make a hole with a cocktail stick for a jump ring, then leave the piece to air dry or put it in a dehydrator for 10 to 30 minutes. When it is ready for the next stage, it should feel slightly warm and leave a little condensation on a mirror.

6

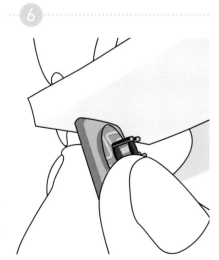

Choose a medium-grade emery board or piece of sanding pad and gently smooth the edges. If the setting falls out, apply a little silver paste for reinforcement when you replace it.

7

Put the workpiece on a rubber block and make a hole with a drill bit in a pin vise where the original pilot mark was made with the cocktail stick.

8

Refer to steps 10 and 11 on page 81 for directions on firing and finishing. Insert the stone and ensure it is flat and level, then use a claw-setting tool to push the prongs over the stone.

PRO TIP

Oil paste can be used instead of silver paste to create a very strong bond when glueing pieces together, and can also be used for cracks and repairs. It is thicker and can be made by adding 25–30 drops of oil to a container of silver paste.

FIRING A CUBIC ZIRCONIA INTO CLAY

SKILL LEVEL

Beginner/Intermediate

WHAT YOU NEED

- Precious Metal Clay or Art Clay Silver
- Stone
- Nonporous surface
- Playing cards
- Roller
- Olive oil
- Sanding pad or emery board
- Silver paste and paintbrush
- Scalpel or tissue blade
- Drinking straw or similar
- Pencil
- Pin vise
- 1mm drill bit with 3mm setting burr, or 1mm, 2mm, and 3mm drill bits
- Blu-tack
- Cocktail sticks
- Dehydrator (optional)
- Q-tips
- Torch, firebricks, safety goggles
- Digital kitchen timer
- Brass brush

1 Decide whether to use one thick layer of clay or two thinner layers, then roll out and texturize the clay. Sand the edges using a sanding pad or emery board before construction (access to awkward areas and angles is easier at this stage).

2 If you're using two layers, connect them together using a little water on the front of the bottom layer and apply silver paste to the reverse of the smaller piece.

3

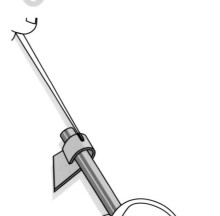

To make a bail, roll out and texture some clay and cut it to shape with a scalpel or tissue blade. This bail will need at least ¹³⁄₆₄in (5mm) of clay to attach it to the main workpiece. Wrap a section of the clay around an oiled needle file, drinking straw, or burr shaft to make a tube; the direction of this wrap can be from the front over to the back or vice versa. Leave it to dehydrate for 10 to 30 minutes.

4

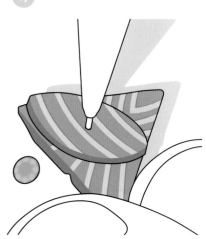

Decide where you want to set the stone and mark the spot with a pencil. The following are two different methods to ensure that the stone is accurately housed:

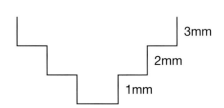

3mm
2mm
1mm

a. Make a hole all the way through the clay with a 1mm drill bit held in a pin vise. Half drill this hole with a 2mm drill, then create a seat with a 3mm drill bit drilled shallowly into the top section of the workpiece.

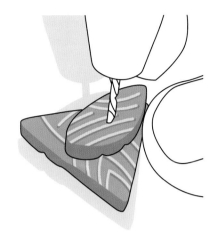

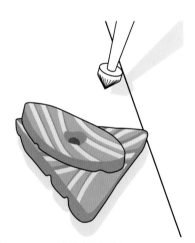

b. Use a 1mm drill bit held very vertically in a pin vise to create a hole all the way through the piece. Then put a 3mm bearing cutter in the pin vise and cut a conical shape, mimicking the shape of the stone's pavilion.

The table of the stone must be flush with the surface of the clay after firing.

5

Apply a drop of silver paste into the setting and insert the stone. Adjust the stone with a cocktail stick until it is level, then leave to dry.

6

Remove the bail from the dehydrator and sand the edges. Paint a little paste onto the part of the bail that will attach to the workpiece, adhere together, and leave to dry.

7

Use a Q-tip to remove any silver dust from the stone.

8

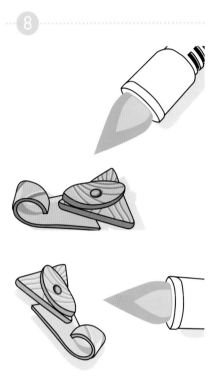

Turn off the room lights and put safety goggles on. Place the workpiece on a firebrick, with another brick on its end set behind, and light the torch to a medium flame that is around 2–3in (5–7cm) long. Keep the tip of the pale blue cone of the flame on the surface of the piece. Move the flame around to avoid any areas overfiring; fire thicker areas for longer than thinner ones. The workpiece will smoke, then, as the binders in the clay start to burn, the piece will create a small flame. This is perfectly safe. A dark brown surface will appear, then an even white color, followed by a glowing orange. Once this temperature is achieved, it needs to be maintained for three minutes.

9

Leave the piece to cool, then finish with a brass brush and soapy water.

GALLERY

OPPOSITE PAGE

Top: Rubies bezel-set in fine silver PMC, with garnet beads. Earrings by Vickie Simons.

Bottom left: Fire opal set in an antique button mold in PMC. Pendant by Kristan Hanson.

Bottom middle: Synthetic sapphires flush-set in fine silver PMC. Pendant by Janice Heaton.

Bottom right: Spinels set in PMC. Earrings by Kristan Hanson.

THIS PAGE
Orange cubic zirconia bezel-set in fine silver PMC. Pendant by Vickie Simons.

CHAPTER 6
BEZEL, RUB-OVER, OR CABOCHON SETTING

This style of setting traditionally houses a cabochon stone, and is known as "rub-over" because a border of metal is gently pushed around the edge of the stone to hold it in place. Bezel strip is used for this border, which is very thin (usually less than $\frac{1}{32}$in/0.5mm) and $\frac{12}{64}$in (5mm) or $\frac{1}{8}$in (3mm) in height. Its purity makes it very soft. Because it is so thin and pure, the bezel strip is susceptible to melting or bending during the making process, but it curves beautifully around the stone during the setting process.

This versatile technique can also be used to set faceted stones, wood, pebbles, shells, buttons, resins, and paper. The method is made much easier if the piece is flat on the reverse; when using natural materials, this can be achieved by gently using a hand file to create a flat surface.

READY-MADE SETTINGS

Although these settings can be bought ready-made, it is much more challenging and your skills will improve more quickly if you make your own.

STONES AND METALS

Traditionally-cut cabochon stones and any stone with a flat base are suitable. The bezel strip exerts very little pressure on the stone so anything from a soft, affordable flawed stone such as turquoise, lapis lazuli, and amber to a more expensive, hard gem, such as ruby and sapphire, can be used. Silver, 9K, or 18K gold are good metals to use with this technique.

BEZEL SETTING

SKILL LEVEL

Beginner

WHAT YOU NEED

- Cabochon stone
- Bezel strip or sheet metal
- Sheet metal for base of setting
- Thin wire
- Dividers
- Round nose or D-shape pliers
- Triblet
- Metal-headed hammer
- Hand file and needle files
- Tin snips
- Piercing saw
- Fine emery paper
- Soldering equipment
- Binding wire
- Ring clamp
- Setting tool (flat-faced)
- Burnisher
- Finishing and polishing tools

1

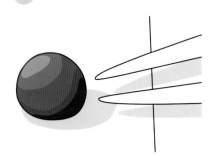

Establish the height of the setting wall by holding a pair of dividers next to the stone, ensuring the bottom point of the dividers is flat with the bench top. Set the dividers to two-thirds of the height of the stone or where the shape of the stone begins to curve. Score this reading along the bezel strip, resting one arm of the dividers against an edge of the strip to ensure a parallel line is scored.

2

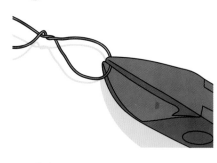
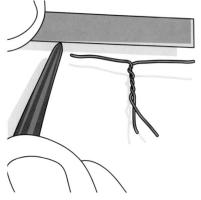
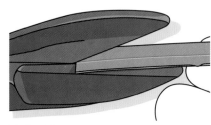

To find the circumference of the stone, wrap a piece of scrap wire around the base of the stone and twist it together tightly to form a loop. Snip the loop apart at the other side to the twist and straighten the wire. Mark this length against the bezel strip, giving the approximate length required for the setting. Cut with tin snips, ensuring the cuts remain on the outside of the lines.

Make the bezel strip round using round-nose or D-shape pliers. It should be just too small for the stone to fit inside (the stone should sit on top of the setting at this stage), with a slight overlap of metal.

Flux and solder the bezel strip together using hard solder. Sit the setting on the solder and use the torch to draw it upward through the overlap instead of trying to balance the solder on top of the join. Squeeze the overlap together with tweezers during heating and ensure that the flame does not linger for too long inside the enclosed shape. Leave to cool, then pickle.

PRO TIPS

If you're working with a tiny stone, use one arm of a pair of round-nose pliers or a scribe instead of the triblet in step 5. Use the tip of a ring mandrel for larger gems.

Prevent a stone getting stuck in its setting before it is finished by lying a long piece of cotton or a strip of paper inside first. Remove a stuck stone by shaking the workpiece in a plastic box with the lid on, pulling it firmly with a large piece of Blu-tack, or gently drilling a hole in the back of the setting and pushing from behind.

If sheet metal has been used for the setting, file a bevel around the top one-third section of the setting using a needle file to reduce the thickness before inserting the stone.

BEZEL SETTING CONTINUED

5

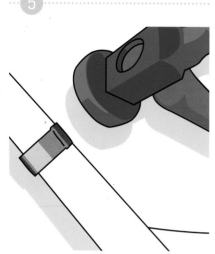

When it's clean, make the setting the right fit by tapping it around a triblet. Put the bezel strip on the triblet, lean the triblet in the V of the bench peg, and gently but firmly tap the soldered overlap using a metal-headed hammer. This will stretch the overlap to become single thickness again, but as the head of the hammer and the triblet are both made of steel, the stretching will happen very quickly. Test the setting for size around the stone regularly, and keep turning the setting upside down on the triblet in between hammering to ensure its wall does not flute or taper. Don't hammer directly onto the triblet as this causes marks that are difficult to remove. Do not shorten the height of the setting wall.

6

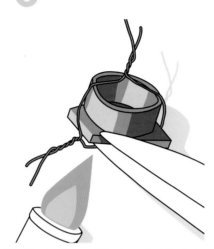

File the bottom of the bezel strip flat and solder it onto the base sheet or the piece using medium solder. Flux, then tuck some solder next to the outside edge of the setting—applying the solder here will ensure there are no lumps inside the setting that could make the stone sit unevenly. A gentle flame from underneath will prevent the bezel strip melting. Tilt the piece and use the torch to trace the shape of the base of the setting to encourage the solder to flow horizontally around the join. Use binding wire to stop the setting slipping during soldering.

7

Once it's clean, cut off the excess metal around the outside of the setting using a piercing saw. Neaten and file true with a needle file and emery paper. Don't push the stone in at this stage: further soldering, pickling, and finishing will damage it.

8

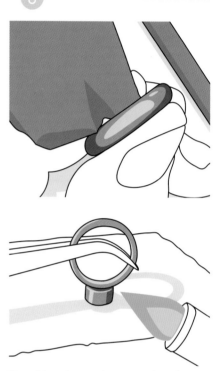

To solder the setting onto the piece, place the setting upside down on a firebrick, find the join in the shank, and file a small flat area at the opposite side to the solder join. This ensures the easy solder in between the setting and the piece has a maximum surface area so will be strong if knocked, it also lessens the likelihood of the other solder join in the piece coming open during reheating. Pickle, finish, and polish. Secure the piece in setters cement, a ring clamp, or against a piece of wood.

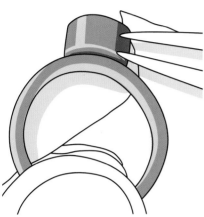

Measure approximately two-thirds of the height of the stone with dividers and scribe a line around the top of the setting by resting one arm of the dividers against the base of the setting to ensure a parallel line is scribed around the top edge. Trim the excess metal with tin snips, then use a file and emery paper along the top of the setting to make it horizontal. Remove any obstructions inside the setting.

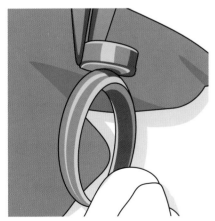

The edges of the setting might need to be retrued using D-shape pliers. If the base of the stone is not completely flat, insert a circular shoulder of wire into the setting.

Place the stone so that any inclusions and patterns look at their best.

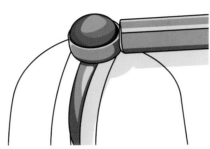

If the stone fits well, secure it in position by using a setting tool from the front and stabilizing from the back with the bench peg in the north and south, then east and west points. This anchors the stone and ensures it won't fall out. Gently push the metal over using the setting tool first at a horizontal angle and then bringing the tool upward until it is almost vertical, until the stone feels firm. This can be tested by running a fingertip gently across the surface of the stone, or pulling at it with a piece of Blu-tack.

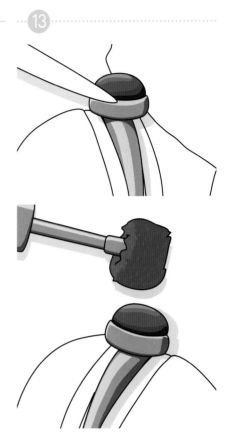

Gently emery paper out any marks created by the setting tool. Give the setting a final polish with a burnishing tool, barrel polisher, or mops on the polisher or in the pendant motor.

GALLERY

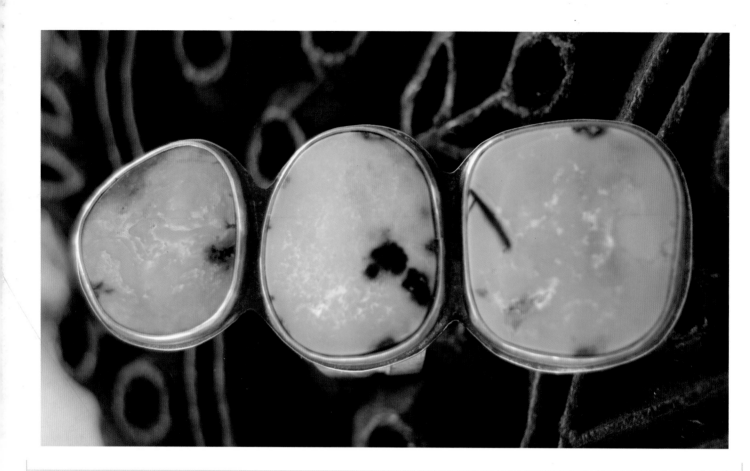

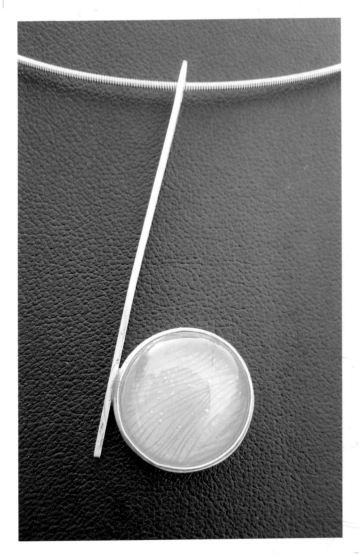

OPPOSITE PAGE

Top: Bezel-set turquoise ring by Christine Bartoletta.

Bottom left: Titanium-diffused quartz druzy bezel set in oxidized silver. Ring by Celia Boaz.

Bottom right: Pendant with bezel-set stone by Alan Ardiff.

THIS PAGE

Top left: Bullet-shaped Peruvian blue opal bezel-set in fine and sterling silver. Pendant by Anne Malone

Bottom left: Pink and silver dichroic fused glass bezel-set in sterling silver. Pendant by Lisa Dienst-Thomas.

Top right: Bezel-set prehnite stone, surrounded by flush-set diamonds. Ring by Liaung Chung Yen.

Middle right: Bezel-set garnet in a sterling-silver bracelet by Lucie Veilleux.

Bottom right: Tourmaline slice bezel-set in sterling-silver. Pendant by Tamara McFarland.

CHAPTER 7
TUBE & COLLET SETTING

Tube setting is a relatively quick method, requiring metal to be rubbed over the edge of a stone. As long as the size of the stone matches the dimensions of the tube, any puckering or pleating of the metal will be blended and smoothed during the finishing processes.

Collet setting takes a little practice to perfect, but is quite quick to fabricate and can be adapted for any size of round faceted stone. It allows light in through the stone's culet as the base of the setting is open, and works even better when set in a knife-edged shank. It can also be used as part of a combination setting with smaller stones set on either side.

READY-MADE SETTINGS

Tubing can be bought ready-made; this has usually been extruded so it does not have a solder join, which minimizes problems of splitting, or harder and softer areas being produced after heating. However, handmade tubing can be made from most metals and to a custom size.

STONES AND METALS

Tube: Stones need to be round and faceted; anything above 7.00 on the Mohs scale is suitable. Silver and gold are suitable for finished pieces.

Collet: Any stones upward of 7.00 on the Mohs scale will work. Anything thicker than 1/32in (0.8mm) sheet is difficult to work with. Once you have mastered the basic technique for setting a round stone, it can be adapted for other shapes. Copper and brass are good choices for modelmaking. Silver, 9K, and 18K gold are suitable for finished pieces.

TUBE SETTING

1

Place the stone on top of the tube: there should be some metal visible around the outside of the girdle of the stone, but the stone should not fall down through the inside of the tubing. At this stage, the stone's girdle should sit midway in between the inside and outside diameters of the tubing.

2

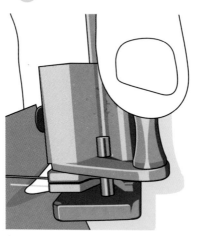

Cut the tube to the length required using a chenier cutter. The tube must be tall enough to house the stone's culet once the stone has been set. Keep the piercing saw blade perpendicular so that the end of the tube that the stone will be set in is straight and true.

3

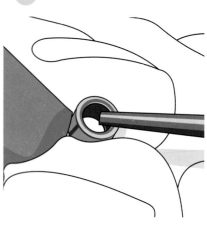

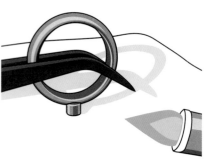

Shape the underside of the tube to fit the piece. Solder the tube on the main workpiece. Take care not to overheat it—trap the flame inside or hold it with reverse-action tweezers during soldering as it will melt and crush easily. Pickle, finish, and polish.

4

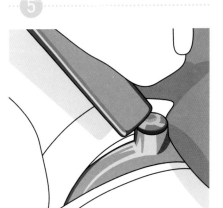

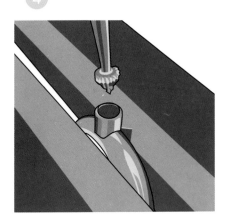

Secure the piece in a vise, setters cement, or ring clamp, and start to burr out the top of the tubing to create a slanted-walled interior cutout "shelf" that mimics the taper of the stone's pavilion. Use a setting burr or ball burr that is the same diameter as the stone. A jeweler's bench drill is ideal as the burr is kept very vertical. You can also use a pendant motor, as long as the burr is held in line to the work. The final fitting and burring should be done by hand using a setting burr or a ball burr in a pin vise. Hold the stone with a wax stick or some Blu-tack and keep checking and burring until the stone's table is flush with the top of the tubing and the girdle sits just below the top of the setting. Gently file or emery paper the top edge flat and check for any variations in the thickness of the setting wall.

5

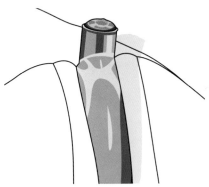

To set the stone, use a setting tool from the front with the bench peg as a back rest to secure the north and south, then the east and west points to anchor the stone. Slowly and firmly use the setting tool from a horizontal position to almost vertical, rubbing the metal over the stone and checking it is not sitting at a slant. Continue until the metal is firmly and evenly pushed over the stone, then pull gently with Blu-tack to check it is secure.

6

Emery paper with a buff stick, polish using a cotton mop in the pendant motor, and burnish around the setting until it is smooth.

PRO TIP

Drill a small hole through the base of the setting inside the tubing before inserting the stone to let more light through a clear gem. When the stone is set, push a piece of wire gently up through the hole from the back of the piece to make it secure.

VARIANT SETTING

Transform a tube setting into a claw setting: mark out four, six, or eight points equally around the top of the tubing, scoring these marks with a piercing saw, then using a triangular needle file to create Vs or cutouts from the metal. Ensure that the girdle will be held, then use a setting tool to push the claws over the stone.

COLLET SETTING

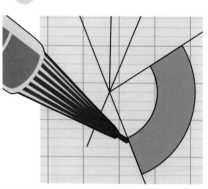

Establish the shape of the collet using graph paper and referring to the template on page 183. Trace the shape and use double-sided tape to stick it to the metal.

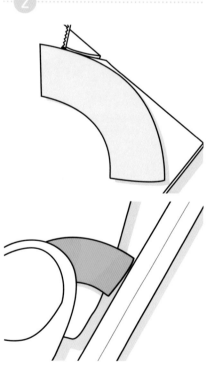

Pierce this shape out, then file the outline, paying special attention to the straight edges.

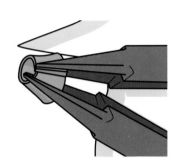

Anneal, pickle, rinse, and dry the shape, then curve it using a pair of round nose-pliers to form the collet. Keep annealing and bending until the two short ends match together, then solder using hard solder. It doesn't matter if the collet is misshapen at this stage, just that the join is very tight. Pickle.

When the collet is clean, file off excess solder and shape it with a collet punch and plate—the taper of the cone will dictate whether a 17-degree or 28-degree collet plate and punches should be used. Place the collet in a conical cutout that it fits tightly into without being too tall, then insert the punch and use a hide mallet to true the piece. File the top and bottom faces and check the collet is true by standing it on a steel block, looking at it at eye level, and slowly rotating it.

5

Solder the collet onto the workpiece, then pickle and polish or satinize depending on your chosen finish.

6

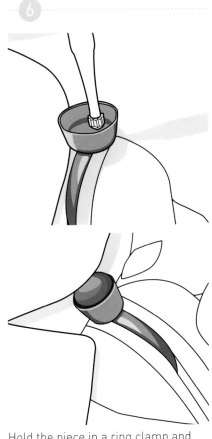

Hold the piece in a ring clamp and use a ball burr in the pendant motor to seat the stone. The burr needs to be the same diameter as the stone or slightly smaller. The stone should be housed in the setting so that the girdle is just below the top surface and a thin lip of metal is visible. (Use a setting burr or bud burr if preferred.) Ensure the stone is seated firmly by holding it underneath the benchpeg and pushing upward into the underside of the wood.

7

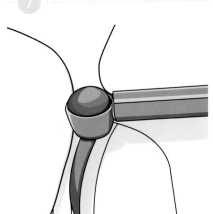

Use a setting tool to anchor the stone by pushing from the front of the setting (6 o'clock) while resting the back of the jewelry (12 o'clock) against the bench peg to create a clamping action. (If you're finding it difficult to push the metal over the stone, it can be made slightly thinner by either reburring the inside or filing the outside top section with a needle file.) Then turn the workpiece to rub over the 3 o'clock and 9 o'clock points; press the face of the setting tool horizontally against the setting, then bring it up to a vertical angle to curve the metal over the stone and hold it in place. If the metal around the top of the setting is tough to rub over, file the top outside to make it thinner. Finish off with a burnishing tool to ensure the stone is secure.

VARIANT SETTINGS

Drill small holes into the tapered sides of a collet setting, piercing stars, triangles, etc. "Claws" can be added by soldering thin, vertical strips or lengths of wire to the outside of the collet that exceed its length at the top. These can be held during soldering by upturning the collet and drilling holes of equal depth into a charcoal block to ensure all the claws will be at roughly the same height.

GALLERY

CHAPTER 8
GYPSY, FLUSH,
OR BURNISH SETTING

The gypsy method (also known as flush or burnish) "buries" a stone into the thickness of the metal, and can be applied to both flat and curved designs. It is a backless setting that displays a faceted stone beautifully and is suitable for everyday wear.

A lot of practice is required to perfect this technique. Repeat the setting using the same-sized stones in the same thickness of metal to ascertain the correct pressure and depth required and achieve the accuracy and precision necessary before working on a final piece.

STONES AND METALS

Small, round faceted stones of a hardness of 7.00 or more on the Mohs scale are suitable for gypsy settings. All alloys of precious metals can be used, apart from fine silver or gold, which are too soft.

GYPSY SETTING

1

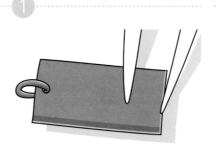

Mark out, center punch, and drill a hole to begin the stonesetting process, ensuring the thickness of the metal is equal to or exceeds the depth of the stone. The hole drilled should be slightly smaller than the diameter of the stone.

2

The workpiece can be held in place using setters cement during the setting process if desired. Make sure the drilled hole has clearance.

3

You now need to cut a seat to fit the stone. Secure a setting burr or ball burr of the same width or just smaller than the stone in a bench motor or pendant motor. Keep slowly burring and checking the depth of the stone until its table is flush with the surface of the metal. Insert the burr in the pin vise to remove any final metal. Keep the burr completely vertical throughout or the setting shape will become baggy.

4

The next stage is optional: use a bearing cutter, which has a 90-degree angle on its sides to carve out a very small ledge beneath the top of the inside of the seat already burred out. Smooth the area with emery paper.

⑤

Use tweezers or setters wax to place the stone in the setting, then push it in at a level angle using a wooden or brass tool to press it into position. If the setting is correct, the stone will "click" into place.

⑥

Burnish around the stone using a gypsy-setting tool or two polished nails, beginning with the less pointed tool first. Anchor the gem by pushing down in the north and south, then east and west points, then use the tool in an upright position with an even pressure exerted to ensure the stone does not tip. By tracing the channel around the edge of the stone using circular motions, the tip of the tool burnishes some of the material inward toward the stone, holding it in place. The more pointed tool used in the same way makes this groove deeper and the stone more secure.

⑦

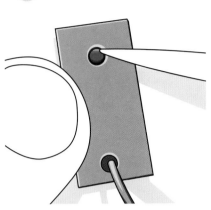

Remove the piece from the cement and clean off any residue using lighter fluid or thinners. Push gently up into the back of the pilot hole to check the stone is held in place, then carefully file and sandpaper out any marks. Polish, then use the tip of the burnisher around the inside edge of the gypsy setting and girdle of the stone to give it a final sparkle.

PRO TIP
Seating the stone with a bench motor is good for this style of setting as it ensures that the burr is kept vertical and at a constant speed. If you're using a pendant motor, try opening the seat by using a ball burr first, followed by the setting burr, as the former stays centered no matter which angle it is held at.

You can make your own gypsy-setting tools from 2mm or 3mm thick masonry nails. Use an old file, emery papers, and polishing mops to create two rounded, smooth-headed tools, one more pointed than the other. Discard saw blades and emery paper after use to prevent any contamination between steel and precious metals.

VARIANT SETTING
Try half-drilling into the metal for a different effect. The stone will only be visible from the front of the piece.

GALLERY

OPPOSITE PAGE

Top: Chocolate diamonds flush-set in sterling silver. Pendant by Erin Staples.

Bottom left: Gemstones flush-set in sterling silver. Ring by Tamara McFarland.

Bottom right: Diamond flush-set in sterling silver. Ring by Andrea Bonelli.

THIS PAGE

Top left: Flush-set aquamarine ring by Lori Linkous Devine.

Top right: Burnish-set diamond pendants by Barbara Polinsky.

Bottom left: Ring with burnish-set sapphires by Sara Lagacé.

Bottom right: Yellow gold rings with flush-set diamonds, blue sapphires, and emeralds by Jennifer Briggs Jenkins.

CHAPTER 9
TENSION SETTING

This fantastic setting style suspends a stone as if by magic, enabling light to bounce around inside it. It is quick to produce, but demands precision fitting and for the metal to maintain the correct pressure throughout the life of the piece of jewelry. As the name suggests, there is an amount of tension between the metal and stone, so any internal features in the stone could cause problems. It is usually only used for rings as not enough compression can be created in a smaller piece to hold the stone.

READY-MADE SETTINGS

The ring shank for this technique can be bought ready-made; the advantage of this is that they are usually cast or extruded, so have no join. The disadvantage is that they only come in a small selection of sizes, so you might need to make some alterations.

STONES AND METALS

Diamonds, rubies, and sapphires are suitable for this technique. Generally, you should not use any stone that measures less than 9.00 on the Mohs scale. Work-hardened silver, white gold, steel, titanium, platinum, and special alloys are suitable metals.

TENSION SETTING A RING SHANK

SKILL LEVEL

Beginner/Intermediate

WHAT YOU NEED

- Stone
- Ready-made ring shank
- Ring clamp with screw base or ring mandrel
- Setters wax or similar
- Piercing saw
- Hand file and emery paper
- Bearing cutter or hart burr
- Finishing and polishing tools

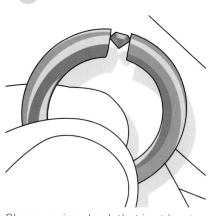

1 Choose a ring shank that is at least as thick, if not thicker than the height and width of the stone—no part of the stone should exceed the edges of the metal.

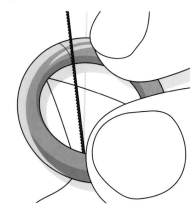

2 Use a piercing saw to cut a parallel-sided gap that is just too small to accommodate the width of the stone (if you're working on a handmade ring, these two saw cuts must be on either side of the soldered seam). Accurately file and emery paper each side of the slot; hold the file straight to remove any marks and to produce a flat, smooth face. Avoid overfiling as this can widen the gap too much or create a curved face.

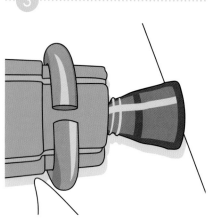

3 Put the ring onto a ring clamp with a screw base and force the shank open slightly—too much and the ring will not close sufficiently to hold the stone, too little and you won't be able to insert it.

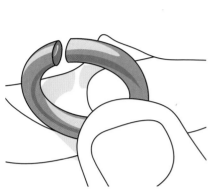

Begin to cut a small groove on the inside of each face of the slot with a bearing cutter or hart burr in the pendant motor. Aesthetically this can be slightly higher than the central axis of the slot when viewed from the side if the shape of the stone will permit, cut in a way that the stone will sit level without the culet protruding when set, and deeper in the center of each groove to accommodate the girdle of the stone. This burring can be difficult in a small gap, so practice on a scrap ring with the pendant motor at a slow, constant speed.

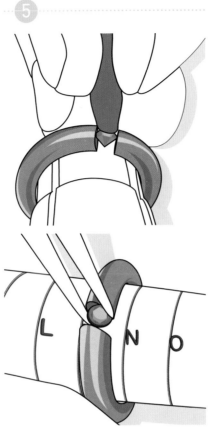

Hold the stone vertically in the slot at the correct height using wax, Blu-tack, or a pair of tweezers, while unscrewing the base of the ring clamp. The ring should close around the stone, trapping the girdle in the groove's cut. Gently twist and pull the stone to make sure it is secure. Alternatively, you can use a ring mandrel instead of a ring clamp with a screw base: force the ring onto the mandrel so that it is temporarily a half size to a size too big, insert the stone into the burred grooves, and hold in place while sliding the ring off the mandrel until the stone is held in place.

PRO TIP

When making multiple rod rings, anneal and wind the rod to form a coil, then cut through using the piercing saw from the inside to the outside of each ring.

VARIANT SETTING

Include a metal bridge holding the piece together underneath the gem so that it appears from the front to be a true tension setting.

GALLERY

OPPOSITE PAGE

Top: Vintage
amethysts
tension-set in
stainless steel.
Pendants
by Kara Aubin and
Daniel Juzwiak.

Bottom left: Gray raw
diamond set in
recycled gold. Ring
by Kara Aubin and
Daniel Juzwiak

Bottom right: Vintage
marquise-cut
diamond set in
hammered stainless
steel. Ring by
Kara Aubin and
Daniel Juzwiak.

THIS PAGE

Cushion-cut
blue sapphire
tension-set in
stainless-steel
"wave" setting.
Ring by Kara
Aubin and
Daniel Juzwiak.

CHAPTER 10
CHANNEL SETTING

This is a variation of a rub-over setting. As long as the measurements of stone to metal are correct and accurate, it is straightforward and satisfying to execute. A channel setting can be achieved on a straight piece of metal as well as curved, and a large number of stones can be exhibited in a collection alongside each other. As the pieces sometimes aren't backless, less light passes through the stone, but the absence of any metal in between each gem when viewed from above makes up for this.

STONES AND METALS

Faceted baguette or square-shaped stones are usually used with channel settings, as their straight edges ensure that they butt closely up against each other. However, round stones in brilliant or princess cuts can also be used, as well as emerald-cut stones. Anything above 9.00 on the Mohs scale is suitable. Use a digital vernier gauge to ensure all stones are equal in size and shape. Cubic zirconias are good to practice with. Silver and gold are suitable metals for this technique. Platinum and palladium are more difficult to bend over the stones, but are more hard-wearing.

CHANNEL SETTING

SKILL LEVEL

Intermediate

WHAT YOU NEED

- Stones
- Workpiece
- Silver rod and sheet
- Vernier gauge
- Setters cement and lighter fluid, or vise
- Soldering equipment
- Finishing and polishing tools
- Setting tool (flat-faced)
- Burnishing tool
- Piercing saw
- Dividers
- Triangular file

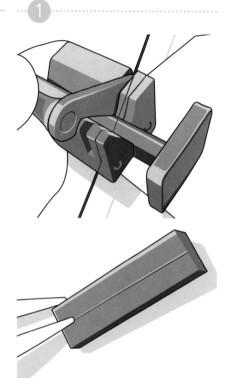

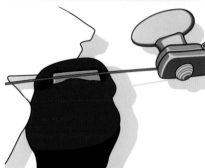

Cut the rod using a tube cutter to the exact length of the stones and ensure all the faces of the metal are true by checking with an engineer's square. Find the center of the silver rod using the vernier gauge and scribe a line along its length. Establish this cutout section by using a piercing saw along the scribed line.

Set the piece in some setters cement or a vise, ensuring there is access for a triangular file to work on the line started by the saw. Keep even pressure throughout the stroke of the file until a V-shaped recess is created and each stone's girdle sits flush with the top surface of the metal. This filing should not exceed the depth of the metal.

3

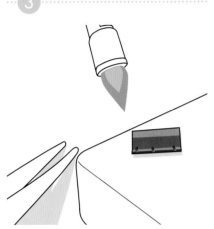

Cut two pieces from the silver sheet to the same length as the square rod and solder to either side of the V cutout. Leave a small ledge of metal for the pallions to sit on and draw the solder through the workpiece by heating from the other side to avoid any solder flooding into the cutout. Pickle, then repeat on the other side using medium or easy solder.

4

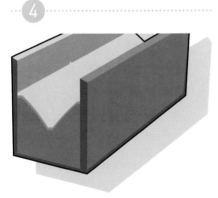

File and clean up all the faces of the metal, making sure the top lips are slightly above the girdle when the stone is in the setting, or so that the top of the lip will run along the edge of the stone's table when it is burnished over. Solder the setting onto the piece, or solder on a bail using easy solder to make a pendant.

5

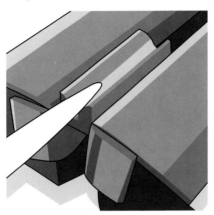

Replace the piece in some setters cement (build this up along the short ends of the square-section rod to prevent the stones falling out) or vise. The following are three ways to push the metal over the stones:

a. File away approximately half of the thickness of the metal from the top 1mm section of the *outside* face of each lip to create a bevelled edge.

b. File away approximately half of the thickness of the metal from the top 1mm section of the *inside* face of each lip to create a bevelled edge.

c. Create a cutout seat where the girdles will sit using a triangular section file or bearing cutter.

6

Place the stones in the piece. Use a setting tool to anchor the stones by rubbing metal over each corner first, then work along the long edges, evenly and thoroughly bending the lips over the line of stones. Use the setting tool at a shallow, horizontal angle to begin with, then apply even pressure as a vertical angle is achieved. Do not allow the tool to rock to the left or right as this will produce gouges. Use even force on either side of these long edges to prevent the stones sitting at a slant.

7

Check the security of each stone by pulling at them individually with some Blu-tack; if there is still movement, continue to exert even pressure along the long metal edges until they are all set. Finish by using a fine emery paper, followed by a burnishing tool or small polishing mops in the pendant motor.

GALLERY

OPPOSITE PAGE

Top left: Black
diamonds
channel-set in
18K gold. Ring
by Liaung
Chung Yen.

Top right: Stainless-
steel pendant
featuring
channel-and
prong-set
diamonds by
Kara Aubin and
Daniel Juzwiak.

Bottom left:
Channel-set
diamonds in
platinum and rose
gold bands by
Anna Bario and
Page Neal. Setting
by John P. Devitt.

Bottom right:
Channel-set iolites
in Argentium
silver. Ring by
Scott A. Fowler.

THIS PAGE
Cubic zirconia
channel-set in
painted brass ring
by Paolo Scura.

CHAPTER 11
CLAW SETTING

This versatile setting style can be used for a variety of stone shapes, including both faceted and cabochon, and although it is traditional to have four claws, multiple claws can be introduced. This style looks delicate but is actually very strong, and because there is so little setting material, a large amount of light can be introduced to the stone from all angles. Depending on the height of the supporting jump rings, the appearance can be that of a tall, sculptural cocktail ring or a shallower day-wear piece. Interesting prong variations can be achieved by using square, triangular, or oval section wires or soldering two wires together next to each other to form a double prong. Variations include a profile of straight sided or tapered claws and using thin or thick wires.

READY-MADE SETTINGS

Ready-made claw settings are available, which are useful for beginners to practice the technique with.

STONES AND METALS

Hard, faceted stones that aren't too brittle such as diamonds, spinels, rubies, and sapphires are suitable for claw settings. High-karat golds and platinum are good metal choices. Silver can be used for modelmaking, but is not recommended for a finished piece.

SINGLE GALLERY CLAW SETTING

SKILL LEVEL

Intermediate

WHAT YOU NEED

- Stone
- Wire for claws
- Workpiece
- Round-nose pliers
- Soldering equipment
- Charcoal block or reverse-action tweezers
- Drill bits
- Needle files
- Finishing and polishing tools
- Side cutters
- Bearing cutter or flat graver
- Snipe-nose pliers
- Claw-setting tools
- Graining tools
- Ring clamp
- Bud burr or ball burr
- Parallel-action pliers
- Piercing saw or side cutters

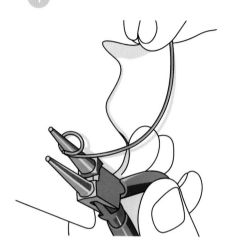

Make and solder a jump ring or "bearing" from round silver wire using round-nose pliers or a triblet, then hard solder it. The outside diameter of the jump ring should be slightly smaller than the girdle of the stone; check this by placing the stone upturned on the bench, place the jump ring on top, and observe from directly above. Pickle, remove any excess solder, and true on a steel block with a hide mallet.

Cut two pieces of wire that are approximately four times as long as the depth of the stone. Straighten and harden the wire by holding one end in a vise, then lean back and pull firmly on the other end with a pair of parallel-action pliers. This will produce straight, true, and mark-free prongs.

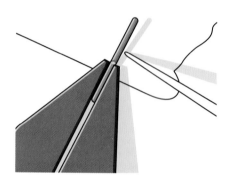

Find the center points in each wire and use a round needle file to create a groove in each piece to reduce the eventual thickness of the cross-over at the base of the claw. This also helps to stop the wires from rolling during soldering.

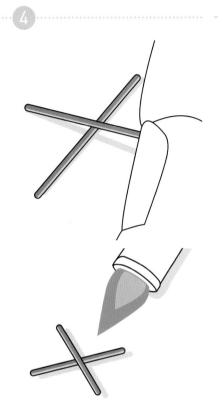

④

Check that these grooves face each other, then slot them together and solder in a cross shape. Pickle.

⑤

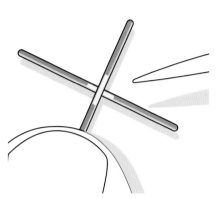

This step is optional: lightly file two grooves diagonally where the wires join with a triangular or square-section needle file. This reduces the thickness of the solder join at the wire crossover, making it easier to bend the claws up evenly.

⑥

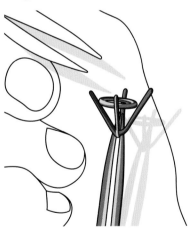

Use snipe-nose pliers to bend all the claws up evenly. Check the jump ring fits inside the "basket" and that the claws are at the desired angle and are equally spaced.

⑦

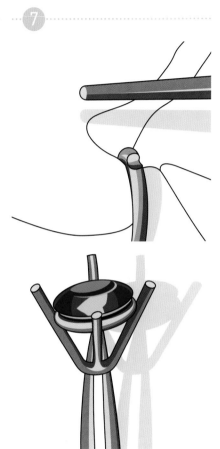

Make shallow cuts with a piercing saw, then use a round needle file to file four grooves with a round, triangular, or square-section needle file into the outside edge of the jump ring at north, south, east, and west points to fit to the claws. This ensures the jump ring is held vertically, is a close fit in the claw structure, and prevents it slipping during soldering. Keep filing and trying until the jump ring fits perfectly in the prongs—the girdle of the stone must touch the inside edge of the claws when it is sitting inside the setting and the claws must be long enough to reach the edges of the stone's table when set. The lower section of the grooves in the jump ring may require more filing to be sympathetic with the angle of the prongs.

SINGLE GALLERY CLAW SETTING CONTINUED

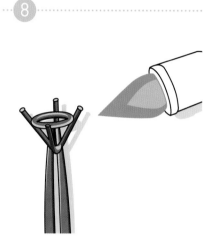

There are three different methods for soldering this tricky construction together:

a. Cut a slot in the bench peg using a piercing saw, grasp the setting with tweezers, and insert the back end of the tweezers into the slot, holding the setting upright. Flux the basket, drop the jump ring in, and attach using medium or easy solder.

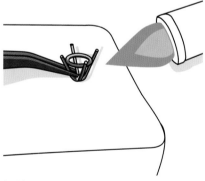

b. Hold the structure upright by grasping one claw in the tips of a pair of reverse-action tweezers. Set it on a firebrick on a soldering turntable, then slowly rotate while soldering.

c. Align the top of each claw so that they are all at a similar height with absolute minimum shortening. Turn the piece upside down onto a charcoal block. Gently push from above or use a scribe to mark where the claws touch the charcoal and drill positioning holes. This needs to be set up so that when the jump ring is sitting flat on the surface of the charcoal block, the upside down basket is true and the claws are at the desired angles.

Solder all four points, complete any further soldering, and carry out finishing and polishing processes.

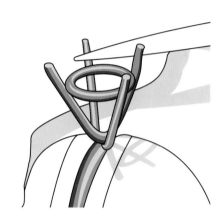

Hold the piece in a ring clamp, and mark the inside of each claw where the girdle will sit and cut grooves using a triangular needle file, bearing cutter, or flat graver. Make sure these ledges are cut to a maximum of half the thickness of the wire in case the claws snap during the setting process. Cut the claws to length; they should be long enough to hold the stone, but not so long that they obscure it. Use a bud or ball burr to remove further metal from the inside of the jump ring to create a slanted ledge, lowering the stone further if necessary.

File the tips of the claws to a point to make them easier to bend over the stone. Position the stone so that the facets are visually balanced with the claws when viewed from above, then rest one side of a pair of snipe-nose pliers down a claw and close the pliers, encouraging the opposite tip to bend over the crown. Finish off with a claw-setting tool while resting the piece against a bench peg until the stone is secure. Gently emery paper and round off the ends of each prong with a graining tool.

PRO TIPS

Use hard solder for as many joins as possible in this complex design. Don't forget that there is a final join connecting the setting to the piece.

Try this technique with a large stone first and use quite thick wire—the thinner the wire, the weaker the claws.

VARIANT SETTING

For a double gallery setting: this style has two jump rings, one above the other. Make a top jump ring as in step 1, then create a bottom second for a claw with a fluted profile or one of the same size for a straight-sided setting. This lower jump ring will sit underneath the culet of the stone: create shallow filed grooves in the north, south, east, and west points and solder into the claw structure first,then secure the top ring. Follow steps 1–8 and remove the underside cross-over tip of the setting before soldering it onto the main workpiece. This style provides a flat base and so offers a more secure connecting solder join.

GALLERY

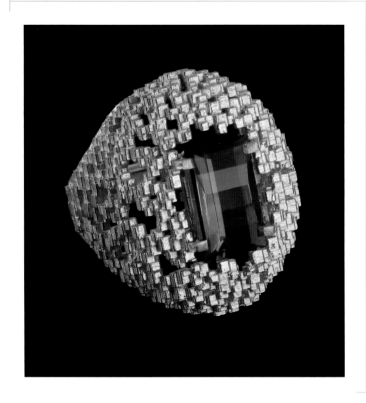

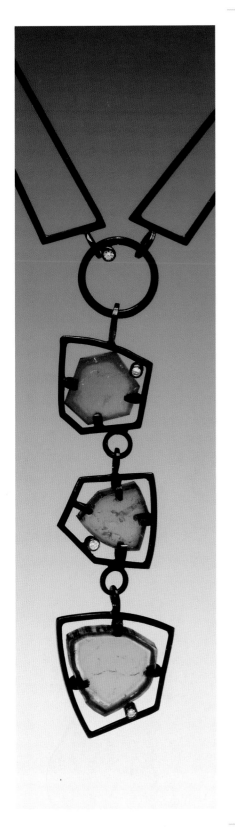

OPPOSITE PAGE

Top: Claw-set smoky quartz in a brass bracelet by Lori Linkous Devine.

Bottom left: Claw-set citrine in 18K yellow gold. Ring by Jo Hayes.

Bottom right: Sterling-silver ring with claw-set garnet by Will White.

THIS PAGE

Left: Slices of tourmaline set in oxidized silver claws. Necklace by Daphne Krinos.

Top right: Claw-set quartz ring by Catalina Brenes.

Bottom right: Quartz cluster held in a sterling-silver claw. Ring by Andrea Bonelli.

CHAPTER 12
PAVE SETTING

OPPOSITE
PAGE
Micro pave-set
diamonds, black
spinels, pink
sapphires, and
emeralds. Rings by
Carlos Orfao.

This style of setting is used to cover an area of metal with a number of closely set stones, tessellating together to create a "paved" look. Its beauty lies in the way that each stone is clearly set off because there is so little metal surround. The effect is stunning when used for covering large, undulating areas of metal, but a pave setting can also act as a flattering background addition, for instance on the shoulders of a ring in a combination setting either side of a larger, central stone.

This technique requires a lot of practice and a number of well-cut stones, which can make it very expensive.

MICRO PAVE

This variation on the traditional pave technique uses a microscope, which means that a fantastic standard of accuracy and finish can be achieved. It is great for setting stones that are 3/64in (1.2mm) in diameter or smaller, and grains can be split two or three ways resulting in less metal being visible and more of the stone being revealed. The physical setup is completely different to that of a conventional jewelry bench: the table surface and chair are low and the microscope stays fixed. An adapted engraver's ball can be used to hold the workpiece, keeping it approximately the same distance away from the lenses at all times and providing easy access from all angles. The equipment and positioning means less physical movement and effort is required, so with practice, speed and precision with all techniques become improved.

The kit can be expensive: as well as the microscope, you'll need a micro motor and a pneumatic engraver. The micro motor has almost imperceptible vibrations so cuts a very precise setting and the pneumatic engraver runs on compressed air and can house different tools to give an accurate, directional, equal force without slipping. As the work is on such a small scale, there are few hand tools available: tungsten steel burrs can be adapted with diamond wheels in the pendant motor for exactly the job needed.

STAR SETTING

This delicate setting style can be adapted to a variety of sizes and shapes of faceted and cabochon stones and is appropriate for curved surfaces as well as flat. It consists of an engraved background that draws the eye into a stone, setting it off without being distracting.The sharper the scorper, the more knife-edged the cut-in points of the star are, catching the light as the piece moves.

STONES AND METALS

For traditional pave: round stones of the same or graduating sizes can be used in the same piece; you will need well-cut, brilliant stones of the same dimensions. Any stones above 7.00 on the Mohs scale are suitable. Silver, gold, platinum, and palladium are all suitable metals.

For micro pave: use stones that are very evenly cut and equal to each other in all dimensions (this can be expensive). The cut needs to be as close to that of the diamond brilliant as possible. Because of the way pressure is exerted on the stone in micro pave, there is a possibility of cracking, so buy extra stones. Any stones above 9.00 on the Mohs scale are suitable, but avoid emeralds while learning the technique. Silver, all karats of gold, platinum, palladium, titanium, niobium, and steel are suitable metals.

TRADITIONAL PAVE

SKILL LEVEL

Intermediate/Advanced

WHAT YOU NEED

- Stone or stones
- Workpiece
- Dividers
- Vernier gauge
- Scribe
- Drill bit
- Ring clamp
- Ball burr or setting burr
- Pendant motor or bench drill
- Flat scorper
- Spit stick scorper
- Graining tools or cup burrs

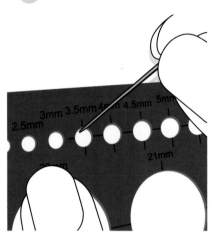

Make sure that the thickness of the metal will house or exceed the depth of the stone. Take a reading from three different points on each stone's girdle to ensure they are completely circular. Put the ring in a ring clamp, find the halfway point in the width of the ring with dividers, and score a line. Then mark three points along this line where the center of each stone will be seated in a way that their girdles are almost touching—too close and the girdles will touch, forcing the stones to sit at a slant; too far apart and the grains will not be able to span to hold the stones. In this way, grains can be raised to hold the outside edges of two stones. If you're working on a large area, use a dressmaking pin in a pin vise and a plastic circle stencil or a disc cutter to draw an accurate guidance grid of circles on the metal.

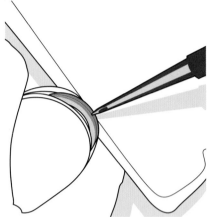

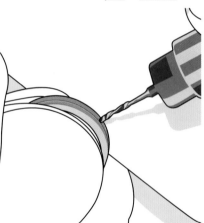

Hold the piece in a ring clamp and mark a small pilot indentation with a scribe to prevent the drill bit slipping, then drill through.

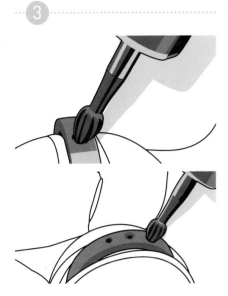

③

Shape each hole to seat the stones using a ball burr or setting burr at the same diameter as the stone or slightly smaller. Keep burring and fitting until all the stones sit horizontally in their settings without tilting and their tables are flush with the surface of the metal.

④

Select a particular setting for each stone. Place them in their settings and check their depth by pushing down on top of them with the handle end of a pair of tweezers.

⑤

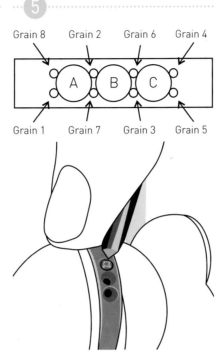

Grain 8　Grain 2　Grain 6　Grain 4

A　B　C

Grain 1　Grain 7　Grain 3　Grain 5

Remove the stones but remember their sequence, then use the flat side of a half-round scorper to raise diagonally opposite grains to separate and fold the stones. Raise the grains in this sequence:

Insert stone A and raise grain 1

Insert stone B and raise grain 2

Insert stone C and raise grain 3

Raise grain 4

Raise grain 5

Raise grain 6

Raise grain 7

Raise grain 8

This process holds all three stones by grain 4, then the other grains can be worked on.

⑥

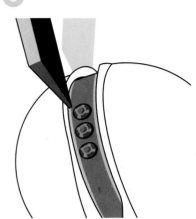

Once all these grains have been raised, use a spit stick scorper to remove some metal background from around the stones, avoiding the grains.

⑦

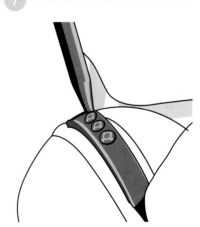

Use a graining tool by hand or a cup burr in the pendant motor in a circular motion to gently smooth over the tops of the grains, creating a mushroom-head shape on each one and embedding the stones.

MICRO PAVE SETTING By Carlos Orfao

SKILL LEVEL

Advanced

WHAT YOU NEED

- Stones

- Workpiece

- Vernier gauge

- Engraver's ball

- Microscope

- Micromotor and drill bits

- Stone-setting burrs

- Pneumatic engraver
  and steel tools

- Graining tool

- Finishing and polishing
  equipment

1

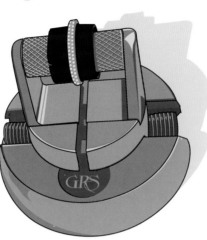

Secure the ring in the engraver's ball, here, I'm using a piece of rubber tubing on a steel rod running through the inside of the workpiece to stop it slipping.

2

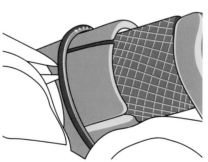

Use a vernier gauge to measure and mark the center point on the ring. Half drill holes using a drill bit in the micro motor. (In this example, I used a 1.2mm by 1.2mm square-section band with 1.1mm round faceted stones and a 0.6mm drill bit.)

3

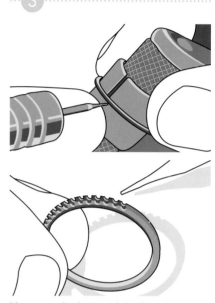

Use a conical, round, ball, or hart burr to open up the half-drilled holes and create seats that are the correct shape for the stones, leaving four claws above the hole. Attach a handmade tungsten tool into the pneumatic motor, and split these claws in two. If you're setting many stones over a larger area, these claws can be split three or four ways. Prepare all settings like this (known as presetting) before inserting any stones.

4

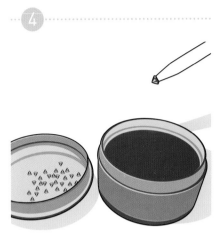

To pick a tiny stone up, dip the tip of an old graining tool, which is spherically concave, into a moist sponge, then touch this to the table of the stone.

5

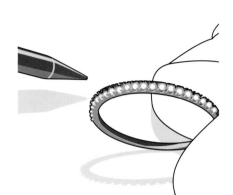

Check that the stone is not sitting at a slant, then smooth over the tips of the claws with an appropriately-sized graining tool in a slow, even, circular motion to create a mushroom-head finish, holding the stone in place.

6

Polish with a burnishing tool or use small mops in the micro motor.

PRO TIPS

The speed of strokes from the pneumatic motor can be altered. Use a slower stroke first for more power, then change to a fast stroke, which applies less pressure and is less intense. Slow strokes create depth to a cut, while fast strokes clean, compact, and finish the metal.

Hold a graining tool in a wooden handle in the palm of your hand and use a slow, circular wrist movement to create an even pressure.

STAR SETTING By Andy Moulang

1

Draw four lines on the workpiece to form a star shape. The stone will sit at the center point where these four lines cross.

2

Use a pair of dividers with one tip set in the middle point to lightly mark a circle to act as a boundary for each point's tip.

3

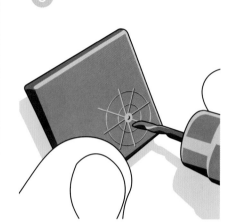

Make a mark with a scribe, then drill a hole through the center of the star. Ensure the stone is shallower in height than the thickness of the metal, and the drill bit is a little thinner than the diameter of the stone. Seat the stone using a ball burr or setting burr that is the same size or slightly smaller than the diameter of the stone.

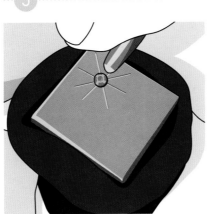

PRO TIP

The length and number of the star points are of the maker's choice. The longer the point, the more difficult it is to keep the tool in a straight line throughout the cut, and can overwhelm a small stone. As a general guide, a point length of two thirds the diameter of the stone is appropriate.

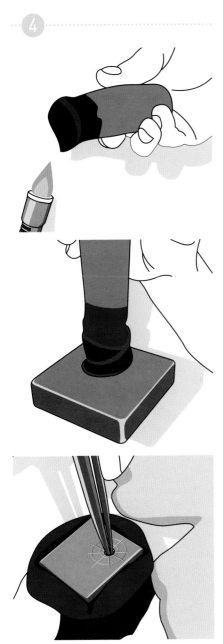

When the cement is cold, insert the stone. Check the scorper is sharp and start at the tip of the north point of the star shape at the distance away from the stone that was made by the dividers in step 1. With the tool at a shallow angle, push it toward the stone to cause a straight parting in the metal, then change the angle of the tool to a more vertical one as it touches the stone. The tool should go slightly deeper into the metal as it approaches the stones. Repeat for the south, east, and west points, then work on the northeast, southwest, southeast, and northwest points until the stone is held with a thin, fine border of metal gathered and parted by the scorper. The last four lines can be shallower as they are for decorative purposes only.

When the stone is set, remove the piece from the cement by wafting a bushy flame lightly over the surface while pulling it gently with a pair of tweezers. Remove excess cement with thinners and finish the piece.

Warm the setters cement with a bushy flame. Make sure the workpiece is flat and evenly installed in the cement. While the cement is warm, check that the drilled hole is clear by using the points of some tweezers or the tip of a bud burr.

GALLERY

OPPOSITE PAGE

Top: Micro-pave set diamond ring by Barbara Polinski.

Bottom left: Micro-pave set diamonds in a platinum ring by Zoe Harding.

Bottom right: Pave-set diamond ring by Katrina Kelly.

THIS PAGE

Left: Pave-set diamonds in yellow gold. Necklace by Corinne Hamak, stone setting by Carlos Orfao.

Top right: Claw-set yellow diamond with cognac-brown pave-set diamonds. Ring by Zoe Harding.

Bottom right: Pave-set diamond necklace by Jennifer Briggs Jenkins.

CHAPTER 13
WRAPPING BEADS
& STRINGING PEARLS

WIREWORK

The first tutorials in this chapter involve basic wirework using pliers and wire cutters. Although these techniques require precision, they are quite quick to produce and do not require soldering. Drilled pieces as well as traditionally-cut stones can be used and the minimal use of wire enables the piece to be set off from all angles.

Wire wrapping is a freestyle wirework technique, which creates sculptural and ornate-looking pieces. The wire used is a soft, nickel-free, silver-plated wire, so it is better not to barrel polish the pieces to avoid removing the plate. This wire can be bruised easily, so it is difficult to achieve a high standard of finish. The wire ends need to be well tucked in so that they don't catch.

STONES, BEADS, AND METALS

Any stones and beads are suitable for wirework, but check that your beads are not too soft and do not have flaws. Copper and brass are good metals to use for practicing the technique and for model making; silver, gold, and silver-color plated hobby wires are good choices for finished pieces. Check that the wire can pass through the drilled holes in the stones or beads.

PEARLS

Pearls are produced in many shapes, sizes, and colors. Freshwater-cultured (or farmed) pearls are the most common type and are in the more affordable price range. They are usually created by pearl oysters, although any shelled mollusk can produce some kind of pearl. Saltwater-cultured pearls are more expensive than freshwater-cultured pearls due to the maintenance and harvesting risks involved in their production.

PEARL QUALITIES

There are six factors to consider when buying pearls, otherwise known as the "make":

LUSTER AND ORIENT: The former is the light and dark within a pearl's shine giving it a depth and the illusion of a ball and the latter term describes the rainbow-like iridescent play of color across the surface. These can be judged by the quality of the reflections.

NACRE THICKNESS: The thicker the nacre in relation to the size of the nucleus (in the case of cultured pearls), the superior the luster and orient, and the less likely it is to chip off during wear.

COLOR: Natural, vibrant hues with a depth should be visible. There should be a "body color," (white, cream, black, etc), with an "overtone" or tint to complement and set off the main color. Artificial coloring methods include dyeing, bleaching, and using heat.

SURFACE FLAWS: A number of blemishes and pimples are to be expected (with the exception of very expensive pearls) but these can be minimized by avoiding contact with perfume, perspiration, and cosmetics. Check the pearl in different types of light and roll between thumb and forefinger at eye level to feel for bumps.

SHAPE: A string of pearls should be well matched to each other and balanced in size. Truly round pearls are the most expensive, with irregular pearls at the lower end of the scale. Some thick nacre pearls can have facets cut into them.

SIZE: Priced by either carat weight or length and width measurements, a larger pearl does not necessarily mean it is more expensive as the purity is governed by the size of the initial nucleus embedded and the nacre thickness. The longer a pearl is inside the mollusk, the thicker the nacre, the better its quality, and the longer it will last.

When you're buying a string of graduating or nongraduating pearls, check that all the drilled holes are central and the pearls are matched in luster and orient, nacre thickness, color, surface, shape, and size.

PEARL STRUCTURES

ROUND: The most expensive as they require accuracy in the irritant implantation procedure. Off-round and drop shapes can be grown and are also expensive.

BAROQUE: Any pearl that is not round and has an interesting shape. Asymmetrical baroque pearls are more affordable than the symmetrical variety.

BUTTON: A type of symmetrical pearl. Useful for pairs.

POTATO AND RICE: These are grown at speed and are at the lower end of the price range. They often have a ridged and pitted surface, caused by the nacre growing at irregular rates, and the luster can be unimpressive.

FANCY SHAPES: These are created when two or three pearls join together to form an unusual shape. Each one is unique in color and form.

MATERIALS AND TOOLS FOR STRINGING

Any type of pearl can be used, as long as they are not so small that they might break during the stringing process. Any bead should also be suitable, but check that there aren't flaws or weaknesses that will cause the bead to chip with wear. Use clasps and gimp of silver or gold to prevent irritation to skin, but avoid fine silver as it is too soft.

Silks for stringing are available in a large array of colors. When matching silk diameter to the pearl or bead, a good rule of thumb is as follows: the thread number should roughly correspond to the bead diameter, for example, No.6 thread can be used with a 6mm stone, but No.5 or No.7 thread should also be a good size. Check by sliding a bead onto the thread—there should be slight resistance without too much force needed to pass it along the silk.

A beading tool greatly speeds up the stringing process and creates neat, tight knots, although a pair of clean, sharp surgical steel tweezers also work well .

BEADING WITH WIRE

SKILL LEVEL

Beginner

WHAT YOU NEED

- Beads
- Round-nose and snipe-nose pliers
- Thin round wire
- Wire cutters
- Clasp

1 Cut lengths of approximately 2in (5cm) of wire, depending on the size of the beads, one length per bead.

2

Measure approximately ½in (1cm) down the length of the wire and form a loop using round-nose pliers.

3

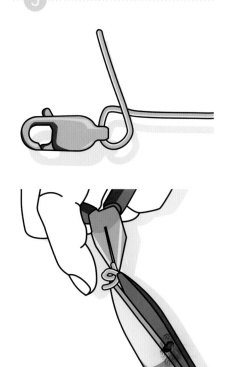

Pass a clasp or finding into this loop, and twist the short length of wire around the long one while holding the loop flat in the jaws of the snipe-nose pliers. A couple of neat, tight twists should be enough. Snip off any excess wire and tuck this end in around the central wire using the tips of the snipe-nose pliers.

Add a bead. Form a second loop in the wire using round-nose pliers, leaving a distance in the wire between the bead and the pliers of around ⅛in (3mm). Hold this second loop flat with snipe-nose pliers and twist the short end of the wire a couple of times around the long end in the direction of the bead. Finish off the end of the wire as before.

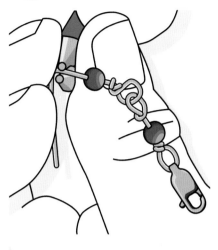

Take a second length of wire, measure approximately ½in (1cm) down the length, and form a loop using round-nose pliers. Insert this second component in through the second loop of the previous link before twisting shut, adding a second bead, forming and closing the fourth loop.

6

Continue until the desired chain length is reached, then add a clasp through the last loop before twisting shut.

PRO TIPS

Add a thin layer of masking tape or FingerPro around the plier's jaws to avoid bruising the wire.

Try alternating beads with metal hollow forms or sections of tubing.

WIRE WRAPPING A CUFF RING

SKILL LEVEL

Beginner/Intermediate

WHAT YOU NEED

- Beads
- Silver-color plated wire, (square and D-shaped sections)
- Wire cutters
- Beading mat
- Masking tape
- D-shape pliers
- Snipe-nose pliers
- Round-nose pliers
- Ring mandrel
- Pencil
- Pin vise

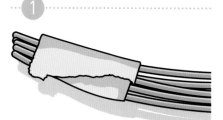

1 Cut five lengths of the square-section wire using wire cutters, approximately 12in (30cm) in length. Once you've mastered this technique, you can achieve great effects using different numbers of wires, but for now, keep the numbers odd (you'll need a minimum of three wires). Straighten the wires to remove any kinks and bends. Lie the wires next to each other and tape them together at both ends and at intervals throughout the length, ensuring that they remain flat against each other without becoming twisted.

2 Cut approximately 4in (10cm) of D-shaped wire. Wrap this tightly around the central section of the bundle to prevent the longer wires from overlapping each other.

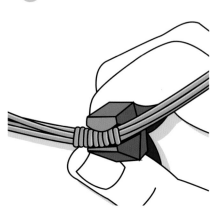

3 Use D-shape pliers to start bending the bundle into a circle, then wrap it around a wooden ring mandrel.

4

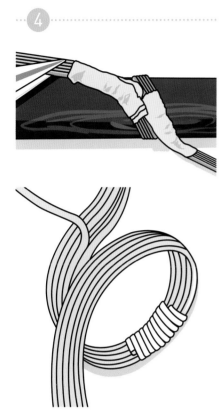

Make the two ends sweep past each other, then bend the central wire up at 90 degrees—this is the only wire that bends upward.

5

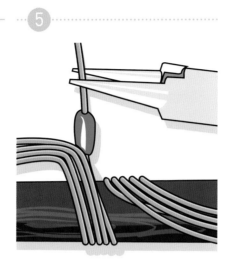

Remove all the tape, add a bead to this upright wire, and secure it with pliers.

6

Add more beads if desired and use pliers to form the ends of the wires into coils. This adds extra decoration as well as securing the wire ends so that they will not snag on skin or clothing. Make sure that all the wire ends are secured and that the piece looks balanced from all angles.

PRO TIPS

You can open up the hole through a bead using a drill secured in a pin vise.

Finish off all wrapping and shaping before cutting the wires as longer lengths enable more leverage.

WIRE WRAPPING A SIZED RING

SKILL LEVEL

Beginner/Intermediate

WHAT YOU NEED

- Beads
- Silver-color plated wire, (square and D-shaped sections)
- Wire cutters
- Beading mat
- D-shape pliers
- Snipe-nose pliers
- Round-nose pliers
- Ring sizer and ring mandrel
- Pencil
- Pin vise (optional)

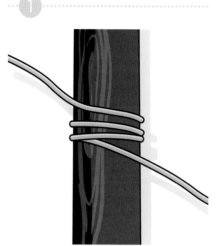

Put a ring sizer on a wooden mandrel and mark the mandrel with a pencil to the size required. Cut a length of square-section wire around 19½in (50cm), find the halfway point, and wrap the wire three times around the mandrel with equal amounts of excess wire extending from both sides of the ring.

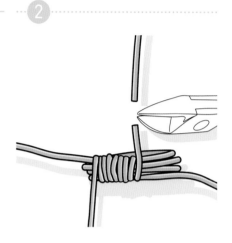

Cut 4in (10cm) of D-shaped wire, fold it in half, and wrap it eight to 12 times around the part of the ring that will ultimately sit in the palm of the hand. Snip off the excess wire and tuck the ends on the underside of the ring using pliers.

Repeat this wrapping on the opposite side of the ring, but keep the two ends of the wires that have formed the shank long without trimming them off.

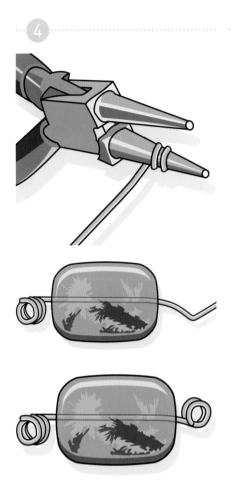

4

Cut around 4in (10cm) of square-section wire, or one that exceeds the length of the bead by 1in (3cm) on each side. Use round-nose pliers to create two circles coiled one on top of each other in one end of this wire, add the bead, and bend two further circles in the other end of the wire.

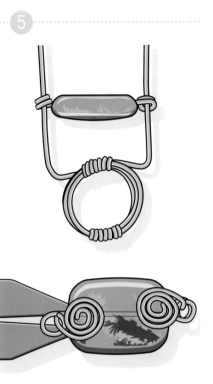

5

Bring the two long ends of the shank upward and slide the bead component onto these wires. Use pliers to create decorative coils or patterns that will hold the bead in place.

PRO TIP
Attach one of the long ends of wire into the chuck of a pin vise and twist for an extra decorative effect.

WIRE WRAPPING A PENDANT

SKILL LEVEL

Beginner/Intermediate

WHAT YOU NEED

- Beads or stones
- Silver-color plated wire (square and D-shaped sections)
- Wire cutters
- Masking tape
- D-shape pliers
- Round-nose pliers
- Snipe-nose pliers
- Pencil

Cut some lengths of square-section wire that will wrap around the central stone or bead, with some extra wire length for decoration.

Lie the wires next to each other, tape the ends together, and wrap the central section of these wires with another piece of wire.

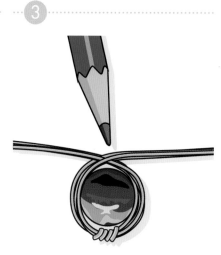

Other wrapped sections usually look best placed on the "shoulders" of the piece at the 2 o'clock and 1 o'clock positions. You can decide where the "cut-in" bent wires will sit over the stone later. Bend these wires around the central stone and mark where they cross past each other using a pencil.

④

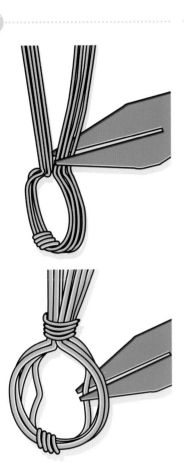

Remove the stone and turn these wires up by 90 degrees using a pair of snipe-nose pliers. Wrap a length of D-shaped wire around the neck— three or four wraps are usually enough. Remove the masking tape.

⑤

Use snipe-nose pliers to bend the outer wires toward the center of the stone to "cut-in" and act as a rest for the back of the stone. A turn of the wrist will produce the kink visible in the illustration here, or D-shape pliers will give a smoother curve.

⑥

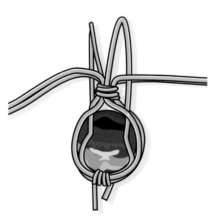

Place the stone into the piece and repeat the wire bending across the front of the stone, ensuring it is set in at the correct orientation and is held firmly in place.

⑦

Choose either the front central two wires or the back central two wires from either side and curve them using round-nose pliers to form a bail. Wrap some of the other wires around the base of the bail to hold it in place, then continue to curve and twist the remaining wires, adding beads if desired, until the pendant is finished.

PEARL STRINGING

1

The silk needs to be stretched to remove any kinks and ensure that the final piece does not lose tension when worn. Unravel the silk, immerse it in water until it's saturated, and tie one end to a weight. Tie the other end to a coat hanger and hang it vertically overnight, leaving enough room for the thread to stretch without the weights touching the ground.

2

Check that the thickness of the silk is well matched to the size of the holes drilled into the pearls: the pearls should be able to move along smoothly without catching or stretching the silk, but should not be so loose that the knots will pass through to the inside of the pearl. The holes can be opened slightly with a bead reamer if necessary.

3

Wash your hands before you begin to work. You'll need to handle the silk a lot, and light colors show the dirt.

4

Cut the silk, considering the length of the final piece, and leaving enough extra to accommodate two clasps. Standard necklace lengths are 16in (40.6cm), 18in (45.7cm), 20in (50.8cm), 24in (61cm), and 30in (76.2cm). A bracelet is usually 7in (17.7cm). The silk will need to be three times the eventual length, with a knot tied in one end and a needle on the other.

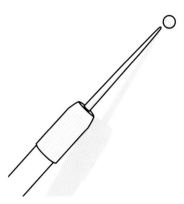

There will be three pearls at the beginning and end of this piece that will require a double thickness of silk to pass through them to add strength and protection from twisting to the immediate clasp area. Choose six pearls, then gently ream their holes to accommodate a double thickness of silk.

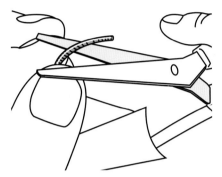

Use scissors to cut two pieces of gimp that are around ½in (1.5cm) in length or enough to house the clasp findings when the gimp is curved in half.

Pass three of the reamed pearls directly onto the silk, followed by one section of gimp and clasp half. Gently bring all the pieces to the knotted end. Pass the gimp very gently along the silk by protecting it with a fingernail—it can easily be squashed, stretched, or distorted.

PRO TIPS

Needles usually come attached to beading silk, but you can make your own by cutting some beading needle wire to double the length of the needle desired, folding the wire in the midpoint, and using a former such as a needle file handle to wrap the wire around and create the eye of the needle. Although it is round at this stage, the eye of the needle will become slim when it is passed through the hole in the first bead. This needle is appropriate for using doubled-up silk: the silk can pass through the eye of the needle before both ends are tied in a knot at the other end.

Making a test thread can help you to work out exactly how much silk you need. Cut a length of silk and measure it, then knot six beads onto it. The actual length needed will be the length of the test thread, minus the leftover thread.

PEARL STRINGING CONTINUED

8

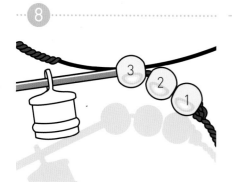

Pass the needle back through pearl 3 and pull tight to ensure the gimp forms a loop containing the clasp that sits next to pearl 3 without any gaps. Pull the entire length of the silk through and tie an overhand knot, making sure that this knot sits tightly next to the other side of pearl 3. Use tweezers to encourage the knot to tighten toward pearl 3.

9

Pass the needle and silk through the second pearl, then tie another tight knot. Pull the entire length of silk through pearl 1, but do not tie a knot. Instead, apply a tiny drop of superglue or clear nail polish to the end of the short tail of silk and allow it to dry inside the hole of pearl 1. This ensures that the tail of the silk will not slip out of the pearl.

10

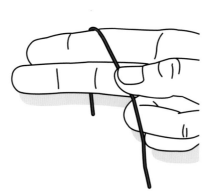

You can now begin stringing the remaining pearls. Start by holding your index and middle fingers straight and together with one hand, with the remaining fingers curled into the palm and have the palm facing your body. Ensure pearls 1 to 3 are hanging down the back of the two straightened fingers, and wind the long length of silk toward your body, holding it secure with your thumb.

11

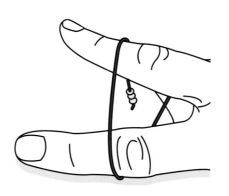

Tilt the hand toward your body while parting your index and middle finger to form a V shape. Pick up the strand of three pearls with your other hand and drop the pearls through the hole in the V to create an overhand knot.

12

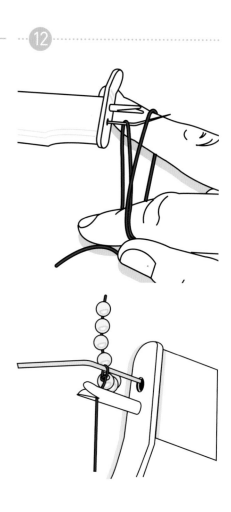

Pick up the beading tool with your free hand and slot the point into the knot. Encourage the knot down the silk until it is close to pearl 3. Hold the beading tool upward and facing you with the silk held tautly in the Y portion of the tool and the already strung pearls hanging against the back of the tool. Push the lever on the beading tool up with your thumb, keeping the silk taut. Slide the point of the tool out of the knot and tighten the knot very closely and neatly next to the pearl.

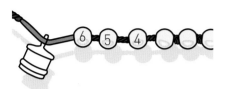

Add a pearl, then repeat this sequence until the length of the string is complete, minus three pearls and a clasp. Make sure the sequence has ended with a knot, then pass the remaining three reamed pearls, followed by the second piece of gimp and the other half of the clasp onto the silk.

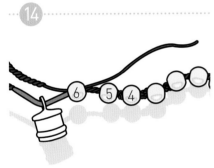

Pass the needle through pearl 6, pulling it tightly until the silk makes the gimp curl into a loop and contain the clasp. Overhand knot the silk using tweezers to help to pull it tight, then pass the needle and thread through pearl 5, overhand knot and lastly pass the needle and silk through pearl 4.

Dab a tiny bit of clear nail polish or superglue onto the tail end of the thread and tuck it inside pearl 4. Wait until it dries, then snip the thread off with scissors very close to pearl 4.

PRO TIP

A pair of matching silver stud earrings for this necklace can be made as follows: choose a pair of spherical, half-drilled pearls and a piece of silver round rod wire that fits snugly inside the holes. The holes in the pearls can be reamed if necessary. Cut the rod into two parts that are just longer than the depth of the holes in the pearls, dome two small silver circles that will cup the pearls without being visible when worn, and solder the posts into the center of the concave side of the domes. After pickling, turn the domes upside down and solder some ear wires onto the reverse. Drill a shallow hole in a charcoal block to house the shorter posts so that the surfaces of the upturned domes lie flat on the block, and hold the ear stud wires vertically with some reverse-action tweezers during soldering. Pickle and polish. Accurately shape and adjust the shorter posts with a needle file to fit inside the pearls. Mix up some epoxy glue, apply a drop to each post using a dressmaker's pin, and adhere to the pearls. Wipe off any excess glue on the pearls using a tissue and stand the earrings upright in Blu-tack until the glue is dry .

GALLERY

OPPOSITE PAGE

Top: Golden Shadow Swarovski crystal wrapped with 14K gold fill wire. Necklace by Celia Boaz.

Bottom left: Blue-glass bead in a bronze bead cap, suspended from a 14K gold fill chain. By Rachel Ball.

Bottom right: Green fluorite stones wrapped in sterling-silver wire. Earrings by Erin Staples.

THIS PAGE

Top left: Sterling-silver rabbit pendant with pearl "tail." By Zoe Harding.

Bottom left: Wire-wrapped iolite ring by Tamara McFarland.

Top right: Golden rutilated quartz wrapped with 14K gold fill wires. Earrings by Erin Staples.

Middle right: Birch wood and glass beads threaded with elastic. Bracelet by Lucie Veilleux.

Bottom right: Labradorites wrapped with 14K gold fill wires. Earrings by Erin Staples.

CHAPTER 14
SETTING IRREGULARLY-SHAPED STONES & UNUSUAL MATERIALS

Once you've mastered conventional stonesetting techniques, you can start to experiment with more unusual shapes and cuts of stones, found objects, and natural materials.

MATERIALS

Various materials can be used, including shells, feathers, glass, ceramics, plastics, fabrics, paper, and wood. Practice cutting, filing, bending, forming, and polishing on some scrap pieces first. Use old tools and blades with these materials and keep these separate from your other stonesetting tools. Clean your files with a brass brush, and wear a mask to avoid inhaling dust. Add temporary masking tape across vulnerable materials to reduce the likelihood of splitting or cracking. Drilling holes in hard materials such as glass can be carried out slowly under water, held on some Blu-tack, and using a diamond-tipped drill bit.

COLD CONNECTIONS

As it is not possible to heat most of these materials, "cold connections" can be employed. These techniques include riveting, where metal pins (rivets) or tubing are run through the workpiece, finishing from the front and back to hold layers of a piece in place. You can also make tabs, small "flaps" or extensions of the piece that simply bend forward or backward to hold a stone in place. End caps can be used by soldering onto the end faces of a ring in place of a tension setting; profiles of any tubing (homemade or store bought) can be used. The set material should sit deeply and securely inside the end caps while remaining visible. It can be held by using pins or rivets through it and the tubing, under tension or with glue. You can also make screws and hinges as cold connections.

Other forms of cold connection include constructing wire baskets and cages, laser welding, and electroforming.

CABOCHON SETTINGS FOR IRREGULARLY-SHAPED STONES

Make sure the object has a flat base to prevent it from rocking in its setting, or fabricate a shoulder from thin wire or sheet for it to sit on to offer stability. Follow the steps outlined in Chapter 6 using round nose, D-shape, and snipe-nose pliers to mimic the undulating edge of the object. Make the setting to size, as opposed to too small. If the object is transparent, the base of the setting can be textured, roller printed, or pierced out in areas.

NAILHEAD RIVETING

1

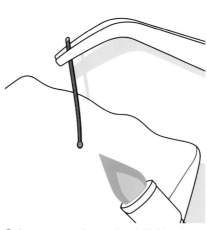

Select some wire and a drill bit of exactly the same size and make a "bead" in one end of the wire by holding it vertically with tweezers, coating it with borax, heating the lowest tip until the wire melts and forms a blob, and guiding the blob of metal up the length of the wire until the desired bead size is reached. Pickle the wire.

2

Mark and drill all layers of the workpiece where the rivet will pass through. Holes in a soft material such as shell can be adjusted with a bead reamer if necessary.

3

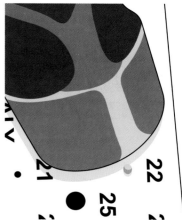

Secure a drawplate with round holes in a vise, pass the rivet into an appropriately sized hole, and use a metal-headed hammer to flatten the bead. A bud burr can act as a countersink to shape the holes in the front plate, enabling the head of the rivet to fit more snugly and be flush with the surface.

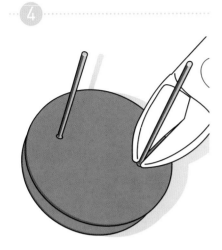

Pass the rivets through the "stack" of work with the bead at the front and place the piece upside down on a steel block. Cut the back of the rivets with a piercing saw or side cutters, so that they are just above the back of the piece. File the ends flat and squash them into splayed mushroom-head shapes using a flat-faced setting tool and a hide mallet.

PRO TIPS
The width of the pin must be exactly the same as that of the hole drilled to prevent the piece becoming weak during wear.

Use paper or cardboard as a temporary spacer within the stack; this can be removed after riveting to allow movement within the piece.

VARIANT SETTING
Blind rivets are soldered onto the reverse of the front piece, preventing them from being visible when the jewelry is put together. Use reverse-action tweezers to hold the pins in place while soldering, and coat the tips of the pins with felt tip or white-out to mark exactly where the holes should be drilled. Double-sided tape can temporarily hold layers in place during drilling.

TUBE RIVETS

SKILL LEVEL

Intermediate

WHAT YOU NEED

- Workpiece
- Flat, drillable stone
- Tubing
- Tube cutter (optional)
- Drill bit
- Setting burr
- Piercing saw
- Flat needle file
- Scribe
- Hide mallet
- Two small dapping punches of the same or similar size
- Steel block
- Metal-headed hammer

1 Cut some tubing with a tube cutter that exceeds the thickness of the workpiece by ⁵⁄₆₄in (2mm). Anneal and pickle the tubing.

2 Mark and drill holes through all components in the workpiece to be riveted. The holes need to be equal in width to the outer diameter of the tubing. Use an appropriately sized setting burr in a pendant motor or bench drill to countersink the holes in the front metal layer of the workpiece if desired.

3

Use the tip of a scribe or a similar steel conical tool in a circular motion to flare out one end of each section of tubing.

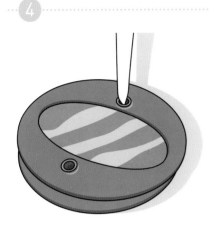

⑤

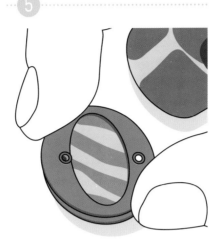

Assemble the workpiece, then pass the tubing through the holes in the layers so that it sits just above the front and back of the piece. Flare out the other end of each piece of tubing using a scribe. Gently file the faces of the tubing to remove any irregularities caused by flaring.

Set the workpiece on a steel block and finish it off with a metal-headed hammer until the ends of the tubing have been completely curled out and sit flush with the surfaces of the piece.

PRO TIP
This is an alternative method to step 5: secure an appropriately-sized dapping punch with the domed part upright in a vise, followed by the workpiece, then a final dapping punch on top, and ask a friend to hold this stack firmly together. Tap the uppermost punch with a hide mallet until the tubing curls open. Finish off by tapping with a metal-headed hammer on a steel block.

VARIANT SETTING
Another method of holding some found, drilled material in place using tubing is to solder pieces of tube that are equal in length and exceed the depth of the material. Clean and finish the piece—try to keep the tubing in a soft, annealed state—insert the material, then use a scribe or steel conical tool in a circular motion to flare the entrance of the tubing until it curls over slightly.

TABS

SKILL LEVEL

Beginner/Intermediate

WHAT YOU NEED

- Stone
- Graph paper
- Double-sided tape
- Sheet metal
- Piercing saw
- Pliers
- Setting tool

1 Make a model in paper or base metal to establish at which points the stone needs to be held, how long the tabs need to be, and in which direction they need to bend to avoid obscuring the best parts of the stone.

PRO TIP

Tabs can be textured, twisted, or sculpted to become decorative parts of the piece.

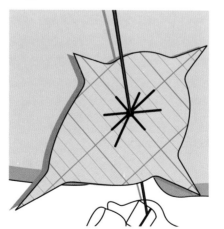

2 Draw the shape on graph paper, then cut it out and stick it on the metal using double-sided tape. Pierce the shape out, drilling a hole down through the center and inserting the piercing saw blade into this hole to cut out the internal tabs.

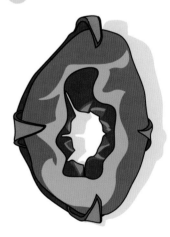

3 Finish off the workpiece, then gently bend the tabs over the stone using pliers, a claw-setting tool, or by hand. Work from the north, south, east, and west points to avoid the stone falling out during setting.

END CAPS

SKILL LEVEL

Intermediate

WHAT YOU NEED

- Workpiece
- Long, thin stone
- Tubing
- Tube cutter
- Piercing saw
- Soldering equipment
- File
- Emery paper
- Polishing and finishing tools

1 Set a tube cutter to the required length and saw through to create two pieces of tubing of equal measurements.

2 Solder the tubing onto the workpiece. Pickle.

3 File and emery paper the open faces of the tubing and remove any obstructions from inside the end caps.

4 Finish the piece, then insert and secure the stone.

PRO TIP

End caps are appropriate for use with durable substances such as glass and wood, and can also be used for materials such as leather and fabric.

VARIANT SETTING

Try using profiles of tubing such as square, oval, and D-shaped to create interest.

MAKING SCREWS

SKILL LEVEL

Intermediate

WHAT YOU NEED

- Workpiece
- Flat, drillable stone
- Drill bit
- Metal to make screw
- Tap and die set
- Machine oil
- White-out
- Soldering equipment
- Finishing and polishing tools
- Piercing saw
- Vise

1

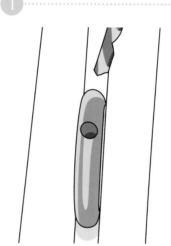

Fabricate the workpiece, secure it in a vise, and drill a hole into it that is just smaller than the diameter of the taps that will cut the thread the inside of the drilled hole—otherwise known as "tapping." Ensure you are not drilling through a solder seam.

2

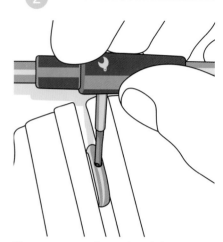

The taps come in packs of three: one has the least amount of thread on it, the next has a thread that is a little deeper, and the third has the most amount of thread cut on it. Put a tap in the tap holder and begin to cut the thread: start with the tap with the least amount of thread and lubricate it with machine oil. Keep the tap vertical throughout, and slowly and gently turn into the drilled hole in the workpiece, reversing the direction by half a turn every now and then to remove any buildup of metal. Continue turning until the tap comes to a stop, then repeat the process using the tap with the medium amount of thread, followed by the tap with the deepest thread. Don't force the tap as it can easily cross-thread the hole or snap in the piece.

③

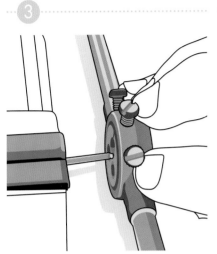

To create the screw, otherwise known as "threading," file the tip of some rod that is just bigger than the hole drilled in the workpiece. Secure the rod in a vise and the die in a die holder. Lubricate with machine oil, then gently and slowly begin to cut a thread onto the rod, reversing by half a turn now and again to remove any excess metal.

④

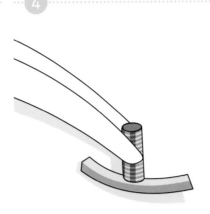

Cut a section of threaded rod from the full length using a saw, then solder onto a piece that will give the user leverage during turning. Use white-out as a barrier to prevent the solder running up the thread on the rod. Pickle, finish, and assemble the piece.

PRO TIPS

The golden rule when making screws is to ensure that one part (either the screw or the workpiece) must be made of a different, harder metal than the other: if they are of equal hardness they will wear each other away too quickly. I use sterling silver for the main workpiece and fabricate the screws from 18K white gold.

The screw needs to be able to turn at least a full four revolutions into the depth of the piece to ensure it will not come undone during wear.

MAKING HINGES

SKILL LEVEL

Intermediate

WHAT YOU NEED

- Workpiece
- Tubing
- Rod that fits snugly inside the tubing
- Ruler
- Dividers
- Piercing saw and blades
- Flat needle file
- Binding wire
- Vernier gauge
- White-out
- Soldering equipment
- Polishing and finishing tools
- Center punch
- Hide mallet
- Steel block

1 Divide a piece of tubing into three sections using a ruler and dividers. Work on a longer piece of tubing at this stage to make it easier to hold. Use a piercing saw to cut out a half-scoop in the central section to prevent the hard solder running into this area during step 2.

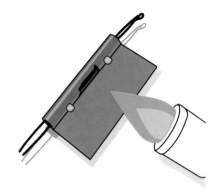

2 File a bevel onto one long edge of the workpiece. Trim the piece of tubing with the scooped-out section to the same length as the workpiece, and match it up to the beveled edge. Solder the tubing to the sheet using hard solder, ensuring that the scooped-out area is facing toward the beveled edge. Run a doubled-up piece of binding wire through this tubing to act as a stabilizer and to prevent it from rolling during soldering. Use hard solder, then keep this part unpickled—the unclean surface will help to prevent the solder from running where it is not wanted during step 5.

Remove the central unsoldered section of the tubing with a piercing saw and file the inside facing edges.

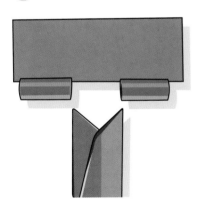

Use a vernier gauge to measure the exact length of the gap left and cut a third piece of tubing that closely fits this space.

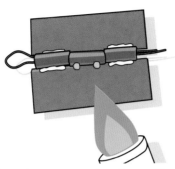

Introduce a second surface with a beveled edge and keep all three sections of tubing aligned by passing binding wire down through them. Apply white-out to the existing hard solder joins to prevent them reopening, and solder the central section of tubing onto the second surface using medium or easy solder.

When cool, remove the binding wire, pickle, and finish. Pass some tightly fitting rod through the three sections of tubing, hold the hinge vertically on a steel block, and secure each end of the rod by tapping with a center punch and hide mallet—this secures the rod and slightly compacts the hinge, creating a slight stiffness when opening and closing.

PRO TIPS

Bear in mind that the angle that the hinge can open is governed by the angle filed.

The tubing is traditionally split up into three parts, but the middle section can be narrower than the other two.

Use this technique to create a hinged box with a stone set into the underside of the lid—a secret surprise when the piece is opened.

GALLERY

OPPOSITE PAGE

Top: Lapis lazuli held in a cage created by joining two 18K gold hoop earrings. Pendant by Corinne Hamak.

Bottom left: Clear glass cabochon held with copper tabs. Pendant by Lisa Dienst-Thomas.

Bottom right: Pink tourmaline held in a ring setting by drilled wire. By Daphne Krinos.

THIS PAGE

Top: Aquamarine, tourmaline quartz, and lemon quartz stones held by drilled wires. Necklaces by Daphne Krinos.

Bottom: Pearl cluster earrings set using electroforming by Ruth Tomlinson.

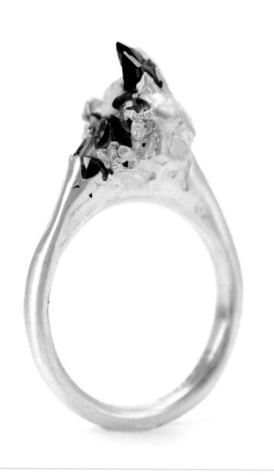

RESOURCES

CHAPTER 15
CARE & REPAIRS

CARE OF STONES

REPAIRS

It is a wonderful feeling to be able to make a much loved piece of jewelry clean, secure, and wearable again. The following dos and don'ts could help to make up your mind whether or not to make a repair.

DO:
- Invest in a studio safe.

- Clarify in detail the damage to the piece, what the client would like done, and have confirmation in writing from both parties before beginning the job.

- Check if the piece has a hallmark and look through a loupe to see what it states.

- Look to see if the piece has been repaired before and if so try to establish when and by whom.

- Look for any plating or parts of the piece that could be an inferior alloy.

- Ask an experienced dealer or setter to confirm the stone is what it is claimed to be before it is removed from the piece. Ideally, it should come with a certificate for proof.

DON'T:
- Heat, cut, clean, mark, pickle, polish, or remove the stone if you are not sure what it is.

- Attempt to drastically resize a ring with the stone still in place. It could crack or pop out.

STORAGE AND WEAR

Each stone has its own care requirements, but the following are general tips for the longevity of a piece:

- Store each stone or piece of jewelry separately to avoid scratching, bumping, or entanglement by wrapping in acid-free tissue paper or a soft cloth and keeping in a dark, dry box.

- Do some research before buying: some stones are susceptible to damage from sunlight, artificial light, moisture, dryness, excessive heat, perfumes, acids, perspiration, chemicals, and cosmetics. Ensure their general environments will be appropriate.

- Most stones can be gently cleaned with a mild detergent, warm water, and a soft toothbrush.

- Some stones, such as opals and jet, need a little moisture during storage. Use a perfume-free baby wipe in a clear plastic bag for this.

- Try not to wear pieces exhibiting very soft stones and very hard stones together to avoid them damaging each other. Do not expose brittle stones, for instance those set in rings, to sudden and harsh knocks.

- Stones of an organic material can absorb dirt and skin oils quickly—wipe with a a warm, damp cloth before returning them to the jewelry box.

HEALTH AND SAFETY IN THE JEWELRY WORKSHOP

HEALTH AND SAFETY EQUIPMENT

GOGGLES: Must be worn, even over glasses.

APRON: Plastic, leather, and fabric versions are available.

CUP MASK: To lessen inhalation of dust and fumes.

LATEX GLOVES: For sensitive skin.

LEATHER GAUNTLETS: For use with a kiln.

FINGER TAPE OR RUBBER THIMBLES: To protect fingertips.

EAR PROTECTORS: For use during noisy hammering.

BEST PRACTICE

ALWAYS:
- Ensure fire extinguisher, first aid kit, eye wash, and smoke alarm are replenished and working. Establish where the fire exits are if you're working in an unfamiliar place.

- Work in a ventilated area when using acids and chemicals.

- Tie back long hair, loose jewelry, and clothing when using electrical equipment.

- Wear closed-toed shoes in case heavy or hot metal is dropped on your feet.

- Eat and drink in a separate place to avoid spillages or imbibing chemicals and metal dust. Wash your hands before preparing food or eating.

- Secure equipment such as a bench motor or rolling mill to a stable surface before use.

- Store chemicals in a dark, locked box or cupboard. Mixed-up chemicals should state the date of preparation.

- Mount a kiln on a heatproof mat.

- Ensure your insurance is up to date and correct, especially if teaching in the studio.

- Turn propane gas off at the bottle before leaving the studio, and bleed the gas pipe regularly.

- Take relative precautions if you're pregnant.

NEVER:
- Let yourself be distracted when using electrical equipment.

- Leave machinery running when not in use.

- Polish chains with a bench polisher, or wear gloves when operating rotary machinery.

CHAPTER 16
REFERENCES

DESIGNING AND MAKING A COMMISSIONED PIECE

Begin by building up an archive of inspirational ideas, sketches, textures, and patterns from a range of sources: books, magazines, your own jewelry, photographs, exhibitions, museum collections, nature, fabrics, architecture, wallpapers, found objects, natural materials, and so on.

If a piece is commissioned it could work in two ways: either the client will supply their own stone (confirmation from a stone dealer that a stone is what the client says it is will be needed), or they would like you to source this—a selection of stones can be borrowed from a dealer on approval for the client to view. In either case, it is important that the stones and metals should be sympathetic to each other in color, durability, rarity, cost, and longevity.

The following should also be considered: the time frame, the wearer's eye and hair color, skin tones, clothing worn if it is for a special event, any other jewelry to be worn at the same time. It can be a big investment of trust and money for the customer, so it is important to listen to their desires.

Work out a quote as near to the start date of the job as possible to get the most realistic metal prices. Submit the length, height, and thickness of the metal requirements to your bullion supplier and they will give you these costs. After a budget and terms and conditions are confirmed with the client, taking into account labor, materials, hallmarking, small changes in metal prices, employing a stonesetter/caster/polisher/plater if necessary, packaging and any postage, a deposit is taken for materials (I usually take 50 percent).

I then give the client a choice of three different designs drawn to scale on graph paper from the front back, top, and bottom, inspired by our initial consultation. CAD is a useful tool for this. One design is agreed upon by client and maker, and work then begins: start by making a to-scale model in paper, cardboard, or fimo, and then in base metal. This practice run establishes the order of work, and is a chance for the client to confirm their approval of all aspects of the piece before the final construction begins. If the piece is a ring, a final fitting before the stones are set is also a good idea.

When the final piece is completed, take a photograph of it. Then it is time for the enjoyable experience of presenting it to the client. If regular communication takes place between the customer and jeweler throughout the making journey, then the piece will be loved and adored ... and the remaining payment can be collected!

Give the wearer full care instructions and be clear on your future involvement with the piece, if any (cleaning, repairs, alterations, remodeling, etc.).

Lastly, offer the idea of making a matching piece if appropriate and keep the customer's details for your records and mailing list.

OPPOSITE PAGE

Prong-set purple sapphire with flush-set diamonds in 18K white gold. Jennifer Briggs Jenkins was commissioned to make this pendant after her client inherited the sapphire from a great aunt.

CHARTS

Ring Sizes

USA/ CANADA	UK/IRELAND/ AUSTRALIA/ NEW ZEALAND	EUROPE	INDIA/ CHINA/JAPAN	INSIDE DIAMETER (IN)	INSIDE DIAMETER (MM)	INSIDE CIRCUMFERENCE (IN)	INSIDE CIRCUMFERENCE (MM)
½	A	38		15/32	12.04	1 31/64	38
¾	A½						
1	B	39	1	31/64	12.45	1 17/32	39
1¼	B½						
1½	C	40.5		½	12.85	1 37/64	40.4
1¾	C½						
2	D	42.5	2	33/64	13.06	1 41/64	41.7
2¼	D½						
2½	E	43	3	17/32	13.67	1 11/16	43.0
2¾	E½						
3	F	44	4	35/64	14.07	1 47/64	44.2
3¼	F½		5				
3½	G	45		9/16	14.48	1 25/32	45.5
3¾	G½		6				
4	H	46.5	7	37/64	14.88	1 27/32	46.8
4¼	H½						
4½	I	48	8	19/32	15.29	1 57/64	48.0
4¾	J	49					
5	J½		9	5/8	15.70	1 15/16	49.0
5¼	K	50					
5½	K½		10	41/64	16.10	1 63/64	
5¾	L	51.5					
6	L½		11	21/32	16.51	2 3/64	51.5
6¼	M	53	12				
6½	M½		13	43/64	16.92	2 3/32	52.8
6¾	N	54					
7	N½		14	11/16	17.35	2 9/64	54.0
7¼	O	55					
7½	O½		15	45/64	17.75	2 13/64	55.3
7¾	P	56.5					
8	P½		16	23/32	18.19	2¼	56.6
8¼	Q	58					
8½	Q½		17	47/64	18.53	2 19/64	57.8
8¾	R	59					
9	R½		18	¾	18.89	2 11/32	59.1
9¼	S	60					
9½	S½		19	49/64	19.41	2 13/32	60.6
9¾	T	61					
10	T½		20	25/32	19.84	2 29/64	62.2
10¼	U	62.5	21				
10½	U½		22	51/64	20.20	2½	63.1
10¾	V	64					
11	V½		23	13/16	20.68	2 9/16	64.3
11¼	W	65					
11½	W½		24	53/64	21.08	2 39/64	65.7
11¾	X	66					
12	X½		25	27/32	21.49	2 21/32	67.9
12¼	Y	68					
12½	Z	69	26	55/64	21.89	2 45/64	68.5
12¾	Z½						

Ring size is not the same as finger size: a wider ring will need to be larger than the finger size. A set of ring measurers or sizers should be used that are similar in width to the ring being made. Always add the thickness of the metal being used to the length of the ring blank.

USEFUL FORMULAS:

Circumference = 3.142 × diameter

Area = 3.142 × (radius^2)

Metal Thickness
Imperial and Metric Conversions and Drill Sizes

B & S GAUGE	MILLIMETERS	INCHES THOU.	INCHES FRACTIONS	DRILL NO.
0	8.5	0.325	$^{21}/_{64}$	
1	7.3	0.289	$^{9}/_{32}$	
2	6.5	0.257	$^{1}/_{4}$	
3	5.8	0.229	$^{7}/_{32}$	1
4	5.2	0.204	$^{13}/_{64}$	6
5	4.6	0.182	$^{3}/_{16}$	15
6	4.1	0.162	$^{5}/_{32}$	20
7	3.6	0.144	$^{9}/_{64}$	27
8	3.2	0.128	$^{1}/_{8}$	30
9	2.9	0.114		33
10	2.6	0.102		38
11	2.3	0.091	$^{3}/_{32}$	43
12	2.1	0.081	$^{5}/_{64}$	46
13	1.8	0.072		50
14	1.6	0.064	$^{1}/_{16}$	51
15	1.45	0.057		52
16	1.30	0.051		54
17	1.14	0.045	$^{3}/_{64}$	55
18	1.0	0.040		56
19	0.9	0.036		60
20	0.8	0.032	$^{1}/_{32}$	65
21	0.7	0.028		67
22	0.6	0.025		70
23	0.55	0.022		71
24	0.50	0.020		74
25	0.45	0.018		75
26	0.40	0.016	$^{1}/_{64}$	77
27	0.35	0.014		78
28	0.30	0.012		79
29	0.27	0.011		80
30	0.25	0.010		

Silver Solder Melt and Flow Temperatures

SOLDER TYPE	MELT TEMP °F	FLOW TEMP °F	MELT TEMP °C	FLOW TEMP °C
Hard	1,365	1,450	741	788
Medium	1,275	1,360	691	738
Easy	1,240	1,325	671	718
Extra Easy	1,145	1,207	618	653

There may be some small variations in these temperatures, depending on where the solder is purchased.

Silver Properties

SILVER TYPE	ALLOY COMPOSITION	MELTING TEMP °F	MELTING TEMP °C	SPECIFIC GRAVITY
999.9 Fine Silver	99.9% silver	1,761	960.5	10.5
958 Britannia Silver	95.8% silver 4.2% copper	1,652–1,724	900–940	10.4
925 Sterling Silver	92.5% silver 7.5% copper	1,481–1,640	805–893	10.4
935 Argentium Sterling Silver	92.5% silver alloyed with copper and germanium	1,610	877	10.3

Gold Properties

METAL TYPE	ALLOY COMPOSITION	MELTING TEMP °F	MELTING TEMP °C	SPECIFIC GRAVITY
24K Gold yellow	99.9% gold	1,945	1,063	19.32
22K Gold yellow	92% gold alloyed with silver and copper	1,769–1,796	965–980	17.8
18K Gold yellow, red, white, green	76% gold alloyed in varying proportions depending on color with silver, copper, palladium	1,598–2,399	870–1,315	15.2–16.2
14K Gold yellow, white	58.5% gold alloyed in varying proportions depending on color with siver, palladium, copper, zinc	1,526–1,805	830–985	12.9–14.5
9K Gold yellow, red, white	37.5% alloyed with silver, copper, zinc	1,616–1,760	880–960	11.1–11.9

COLLET TEMPLATE

- Draw a side view of the stone by measuring the diameter of the stone across the girdle and the height of the stone from the table to the culet. (See the shaded cone in the diagram.)

- Increase the height a little and draw a line (A–B) parallel with the top of the stone. Draw another line, starting at the center of A–B and extending down through the point of the cone (C).

- Draw a parallel line below the point of the stone (D–E) to mark the finished height of the cone.

- Add sloping lines from both A and B, finishing at C.

- Set a compass at the radius A–C and draw an arc.

- Set the compass at radius D–C and draw a second arc.

- Multiply the width of the stone (A–B) by 3.14 and measure this along the arc from A and mark it at F.

- Join C with F, creating the template for the cone.

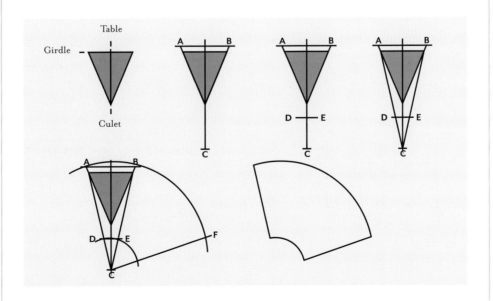

USEFUL BOOKS AND WEBSITES

BOOKS

THE COMPLETE METALSMITH
Tim McCreight. Davis Publishing Co., 1991.

GEMSTONE SETTINGS: THE JEWELRY MAKER'S GUIDE TO STYLES & TECHNIQUES.
Anastasia Young. Interweave, 2012.

HANDBOOK OF JEWELLERY TECHNIQUES.
Carles Codina. A&C Black, 2000.

HOT AND COLD CONNECTIONS FOR JEWELLERS.
Tim McCreight. A&C Black, 2007.

THE JEWELER'S DIRECTORY OF DECORATIVE FINISHES.
Jinks McGrath. Krause, 2005.

THE JEWELER'S DIRECTORY OF GEMSTONES.
Judith Crowe. Firefly Books, 2012.

THE JEWELLER'S DIRECTORY OF SHAPE AND FORM.
Elizabeth Olver. A&C Black, 2000.

JEWELRY TWO BOOKS IN ONE: PROJECTS TO PRACTICE AND INSPIRE, TECHNIQUES TO ADAPT TO SUIT YOUR OWN DESIGNS.
Madeline Coles. Sterling, 1999.

METALS TECHNIC: A COLLECTION OF TECHNIQUES FOR METALSMITHS.
Tim McCreight. Brynmorgen Press, 1997.

THE PEARL BOOK: THE DEFINITIVE BUYING GUIDE.
Antoinette Leonard Matlins. Gemstone Press, 2008.

PRECIOUS METAL CLAY.
Xuella Arnold. St. Martin's Griffin, 2008.

THE RINGS BOOK.
Jinks McGrath. A&C Black, 2007.

SILVERSMITHING FOR JEWELRY MAKERS.
Elizabeth Bone. Interweave, 2012.

MAGAZINES

CRAFTS
www.craftscouncil.org.uk/crafts-magazine

FINDINGS
www.acj.org.uk/index.php/about-us/findings-magazine

LAPIDARY JOURNAL JEWELRY ARTIST
www.snagmetalsmith.org/metalsmith-magazine/about-metalsmith

METALSMITH
www.snagmetalsmith.org/metalsmith-magazine/about-metalsmith

SUPPLIERS

A. E. WARD & SON
Gemstone suppliers based in London, UK.
www.aewgems.co.uk

ART CLAY WORLD USA
Art clay, tools, equipment, and classes.
www.artclayworld.com

ATLANTIC GEMS
Metals, gemstones, and beads.
atlanticgems.com

BEADWORKS USA
Gemstone suppliers based in Norwalk, Connecticut.
www.beadworks.com

COOKSON PRECIOUS METALS
UK-based suppliers of everything the jewelry maker needs, delivered the next day.
www.cooksongold.com

FIRE MOUNTAIN GEMS USA
Beads, gemstones, and jewelry supplies purveyor.
www.firemountaingems.com

METALLIFEROUS
Tools, equipment, precious metals, and findings.
metalliferous.com

ASSOCIATIONS

AMERICAN GEM SOCIETY
www.americangemsociety.org

ASSOCIATION FOR CONTEMPORARY JEWELLERY
acj.org.uk

THE GEMMOLOGICAL ASSOCIATION OF GREAT BRITAIN
www.gem-a.com

INTERNATIONAL COLORED GEMSTONE ASSOCIATION
www.gemstone.org

SOCIETY OF NORTH AMERICAN GOLDSMITHS
www.snagmetalsmith.org

WEBSITES

BENCHPEG
benchpeg.com

CRAFTS COUNCIL
www.craftscouncil.org.uk

GANOSKIN
www.ganoskin.com

INDEX

CONTRIBUTORS

HILARY ALEXANDER
www.lumafina.etsy.com

ALAN ARDIFF
www.alanardiff.com

KARA AUBIN & DANIEL JUZWIAK
KARA|DANIEL JEWELRY
www.karadanieljewelry.com

RACHEL BALL
www.elephantine.etsy.com

RUTH BALL
www.ruthballenameldesign.com

ANNA BARIO & PAGE NEAL
BARIO NEAL
www.bario-neal.com

CHRISTINE BARTOLETTA
www.societyhilldesigns.com

MICHAEL BERGER
www.kineticrings.com

CELIA BOAZ
www.glitzglitter.etsy.com
www.theslyfox.etsy.com

ANDREA BONELLI
www.andreabonelli.com

CARLOS DE PAULA JEWELLERY
www.carlosdepaula.co.uk

CATALINA BRENES
www.catalinabrenes.com

JENNIFER BRIGGS JENKINS
www.JBriggsAndCo.com

MICHELLE CHANG
www.michellechang.com

LIAUNG CHUNG YEN
www.liaungchungyen.com

ELAINE COX
www.elainecox.com

JANNA CULBRETH
www.jacjewelry.com

LISA DIENST-THOMAS
www.LPJewelry.Etsy.com

JANTJE FLEISCHHUT
www.jantjefleischhut.com

SCOTT A. FOWLER
www.scottalexanderfowler.com

MELANIE GEORGACOPOULOS
www.melaniegeorgacopoulos.com

CORINNE HAMAK
www.corinnehamak.com

KRISTAN HANSON
www.silverwishes.etsy.com

ZOE HARDING
www.zoeharding.com

MABEL HASELL
www.mabelhasell.com

EMMELINE HASTINGS
www.emmelinehastings.co.uk

JO HAYES WARD
www.johayes.com

JANICE HEATON
www.jheatondesigns.etsy.com

PATRICK IRLA
www.patrickirla.com
www.etsy.com/shop/patrickirlajewelry

KATRINA KELLY
www.katrinakellyjewelry.com

KONSTANZE KLAUS
www.nodeform.com

EREZ KOVRIGO
www.erezkovrigo.com

DAPHNE KRINOS
www.daphnekrinos.com

SARA LAGACÉ
www.saralagace.com

AMANDA LI HOPE
www.amandalihope.com

LORI LINKOUS DEVINE
www.lolide.com

ANNE MALONE
www.cocoandchia.com

TAMARA MCFARLAND
MCFARLAND DESIGNS
www.mcfarlanddesigns.com

LILIA NASH
www.liliandesigns.co.uk

CARLOS ORFAO
CARLOS DE PAULA JEWELLERY
www.carlosodepaula.co.uk

BARBARA POLINSKY
www.bmjnyc.com

PAOLO SCURA
Paoloscura.info@gmail.com

VICKIE SIMONS
www.jewelflyt.com

ERIN STAPLES
www.erinjanedesigns.com

RUTH TOMLINSON
www.ruthtomlinson.com

LUCIE VEILLEUX
www.lucieveilleux.com

CAROLINE WALKER
www.etsy.com/shop/Scape

WILL WHITE
www.willwhiteart.com

PICTURE CREDITS

Photography is by the jeweler, unless otherwise listed here.

Page 8–9: (Top row, left to right) Elaine Cox, Xavier Young, Paolo Scura, Jennifer Briggs Jenkins

(Bottom row, left to right) Michael Wicks, Federico Cavicchioli (ring by Catalina Brenes), Xavier Young, Liaung Chung Yen

Page 28: Eddo Hartmann

Page 64–65: (Top row, left to right) Erin Staples, Konstanze Klaus, Sara Lagacé, Erin Staples

(Bottom row, left to right) Ian Forsyth (earrings by Ruth Tomlinson), Lucie Veilleux, Tamara McFarland, Jennifer Briggs Jenkins

Page 72: Daniel Juzwiak

Page 77: (Top right) Lucia Rollow, (bottom left) Alyssa Robb

Page 94: (Bottom right) Estelle Morgan

Page 109: (Top right) Don Kozusko

Page 110–111: Daniel Juzwiak

Page 114–115: Daniel Juzwiak

Page 117: Daniel Juzwiak

Page 120: (Top right) Daniel Juzwiak, (bottom left) Alyssa Robb, (bottom right) Lucia Rollow

Page 129: (Left) Joel Degen, (top right) Federico Cavicchioli

Page 130: Paula Vieira

Page 132: (Top) Antfarm Photography

Page 140: (Top) Don Kozusko, (bottom left) Hanover Saffron Creative, (bottom right) Antfarm Photography

Page 141: (Left) Juliet Sheath, Full Focus, (bottom right) Joel Degen

Page 172: (Top) Juliet Sheath, Full Focus, (bottom right) Joel Degen

Page 173: (Top) Joel Degen, (bottom) Ian Forsyth

Page 174–175: (Top row, left to right) Emily Hasell (ring by Mabel Hasell), Hap Sakwa (necklace by Liaung Chung Yen), Jennifer Briggs Jenkins, Ruth Ball

(Bottom row, left to right) Steve Nash (ring by Lilia Nash), Zoe Harding, Konstanze Klaus, Jeremy Johns (ring by Melanie Georgacopoulos)

ACKNOWLEDGMENTS

The author would like to thank:

My thanks go to my family and friends for their support and encouragement throughout the compilation of this book. In particular to Andy Moulang, contributing author, for willingly sharing his knowledge and for all his patience and guidance; to Carlos Orfao for the micropave tutorial; to Jessica Rose and the London Jewellery School for the loan of their equipment; to Cooksons Precious Metals and the skilled makers featured for generously supplying their images, and to Jane Roe at Rotovision for all her assistance.

The publisher would like to thank:

Emma Atkinson for her superb design work and neverending enthusiasm, Heidi Adnum for her excellent picture research skills, and the staff at A.E Ward & Son for their help with the gemstone directory.